DISC

COLLECTION MANAGEMENT

3/04	4	11/03
2/05	8-1	5/05
9/09	17—1	4/09
5/3/12	22— 1	2/26/12

SUNLIGHT ON THE LAWN

SUNLIGHT ON THE LAWN

Beverley Nichols

With a Foreword by Bryan Connon

TIMBER PRESS
Portland, Oregon

Dust jacket photograph of Beverley Nichols is the property of
Bryan Connon, reproduced with permission

Drawings by William McLaren

Copyright © 1956 by the estate of Beverley Nichols

First published in 1956 by Jonathan Cape

Foreword, Bibliography, and Index copyright © 1999
by Timber Press, Inc.

TIMBER PRESS, INC.
The Haseltine Building
133 S.W. Second Avenue, Suite 450
Portland, Oregon 97204, U.S.A.

Printed in Hong Kong

Reprinted 1999, 2001

Library of Congress Cataloging-in-Publication Data
Nichols, Beverley, 1899–
    Sunlight on the lawn / Beverley Nichols with a foreword by Bryan
Connon.
      p.   cm.
    Originally published: London : Jonathan Cape, c1956.
    Includes bibliographical references (p.   ) and index.
    ISBN 0-88192-467-9
    1. Nichols, Beverley, 1899–   —Homes and haunts—England—Surrey.
2. Authors, English—20th century—Biography. 3. Gardeners—England—
Biography. 4. Gardening—England—Surrey. I. Title.
PR6027.I22Z76   1999
828'.91209–dc21
[B]   98-39846
                                                      CIP

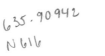

CONTENTS

FOREWORD

IT WAS while having tea with Beverley on the terrace of his home in Richmond that he suddenly asked me if I would like to be his biographer, adding that he would quite understand if I refused. You, dear reader (as writers used to say in more gracious times), will understand my astonishment and delight. After a moment, during which I pretended to be giving his proposal the profoundest consideration, I replied that nothing would give me greater pleasure. "I am not so sure about pleasure," said Beverley with asperity. "It will be hard work, and all that delving you'll have to do may be tiresome but not, I hope, a bore."

Subsequently, during my "delving," I asked him about the people featured in his books. Were they real or fictional? Who was Miss Mint for instance? As I had half guessed, she was really Miss Hazlitt from previous books who had been based on Beverley's governess Miss Herridge. This gentle but formidable lady, undoubtedly one of the most influential figures of his childhood, developed his love of flowers, giving him a sound foundation of scholarship by teaching him to identify them by their Latin and common names. She also showed him how to grow them from cuttings and from seed. He was then only five or six, and in old age he still remembered the wonder and joy he felt when his efforts were successful. It was a sensation recaptured when he created his first garden, later immortalised in *Down the Garden Path*.

I have several of the letters Miss Herridge wrote to "Bev," in which she describes the wildflowers gathered in the hedgerows near her home. These letters demolished my suspicion that, as

Miss Hazlitt or Miss Mint, she was too good to be true. It is humbling to read the words of an elderly lady who believed that her agony from cancer was God's way of testing her faith and was therefore a special blessing.

The flamboyant Bob, who rescues Miss Mint from the consequences of her kindness, was not a member of the Rothschild family as Beverley hinted. He was Robert Lebus a wealthy antique collector who helped Beverley to select at country sales items that would grow in value. Ironically, when he badly needed money in old age, Beverley could not bear to part with his antiques and refused to believe they were worth much. He would have been amazed at the prices they fetched after his death.

Marius was really Professor A. M. Lowe, a brilliant scholar, into whose mouth Beverley was able to place odds and ends of intriguing information that he had accumulated himself. "He was mostly him and partly me," as he put it. The two "leading ladies" Our Rose and Miss Emily need no explanation for we have all met their like in our own communities: well meaning, good hearted, but occasionally absolutely infuriating!

Beverley was sworn to protect the identity of the redoubtable gardener Oldfield, and I must do the same. He gave him the name of the headmaster of his first school, "They were both perfect gentlemen, products of an age when everything seemed certain and everyone knew his or her place in the order of things, and were proud of it."

Arthur Gaskin was very much of this ilk. For forty years he was Beverley's major-domo in a succession of homes. The most romantic story about his background claimed that his father was a valet in the Royal Household and his mother a cook at a great mansion. When he arrived to work for Beverley, he was only twenty one years old, but fully trained in the domestic arts. His skills as a chef were much admired by guests; but despite tempting offers of employment from the likes of Somerset Maugham and Noel Coward, his loyalty was absolute.

The purchase of Merry Hall depended on Gaskin's approval and Beverley showed him over the semi-derelict house with considerable trepidation. Instead of being appalled by the amount of work required to run a house of twenty-two rooms, Gaskin was enchanted by his vision of the renovated estate. Looking at the vast kitchen and the cavernous cellars he commented, "Gives me some room to move around."

During his war service as a sergeant, Gaskin had organised the lives of an assorted group of designers and inventors who dreamt up schemes to camouflage ships, planes and installations. Now he took charge of the restoration of the house as if it were a military operation, and at a time of desperate shortages he had sources which supplied basic materials at sensible prices. His wide circle of ex-army friends were happy to do plastering, painting, plumbing and electrics, and he was also able to summon strong young men to do the heavy work. They were not so much greedy for money it seems, as for Gaskin's endless cups of tea, hefty sandwiches and wedges of homemade cake.

As Beverley said, the miraculous transformation of Merry Hall and its garden could not have taken place as smoothly without Gaskin. Unfortunately, Beverley underestimated the running costs of the property, and he was forced to sell some land and outbuildings, but after ten years of rising taxes and increasing expenses he had to admit financial defeat. He always regretted not seeing the garden come to full maturity.

It was a happier story at his next and last cottage in Richmond where for twenty years he enjoyed the magnificent garden he created out of what was little more than a meadow. A story from the Richmond garden has special charm. Beverley had a myrtle grown from a cutting that was said to have come from a sprig in

Queen Victoria's wedding bouquet. Many famous people visited the garden but Beverley was very excited when a certain princess came to tea and was particularly intrigued by the myrtle. Beverley eventually gave her a little plant he had grown for her. I have her letter of thanks for this unusual gift.

I once asked him why the two books he wrote about the Richmond garden had no stories about people like Our Rose and Miss Emily. This was a sensitive subject and he explained indignantly that he was advised that nobody wanted his brand of whimsy in the "swinging sixties" and it would be better if he left out his "characters." "I should have ignored this but I needed the money. Some argue that the 1960's was a breakthrough for the arts. To me it was more like a breakdown of standards. Writing often became crude and semi-literate, and it was considered old fashioned to aim for grace or wit. As for whimsy, it was condemned as a sort of literary sin." This explains why *Sunlight on the Lawn* is the last example of Beverley Nichols' unique mixture of fact, humour and whimsical invention.

Although Beverley liked to claim that his books were easy to write, this was not true; the ideas came quickly enough but the execution was a painful process of draft after draft (in long hand), cutting, selecting, and assembling, not unlike putting together a bunch of flowers, as he said himself. But his idea of flower arranging was to spend hours recreating the great flower painting of Manet, Cézanne, or Renoir!

It is worth reminding ourselves that Beverley was born a hundred years ago. He became a household name in the 1920's with several best-selling novels and an audacious autobiography appropriately titled *Twenty-Five*. His work was often controversial and he upset the British political establishment by his open contempt for their ineptness. The garden books gave his enemies ammunition and he was mocked and dismissed as a "women's writer," a term of derision when applied to a man in those days.

His appeal was universal as his fan mail proved. Among his papers, for example, I found a letter from an army private written from a combat zone. It was awkwardly composed, but it thanked Beverley for his books about gardens because they reminded him of what he was fighting for. A touch naive and sentimental it may have been, but it exemplified the effect his work had on people around the world.

I was with Beverley a few days before he died in 1983 and, although very frail, he insisted on walking to his favourite seat in the garden. He was in an optimistic mood, chatting about an idea for another children's book and about the foreword he had written for a new edition of *Down the Garden Path*. Suddenly he became introspective. "I still believe the words I wrote all those years ago: 'A Garden is the only mistress who never fails, who never fades.'" Then he smiled, "I suppose today it would be tactful to say 'lover' instead of 'mistress.'" And becoming serious again, "These words may not qualify for an anthology of immortal lines, but I defy anyone to challenge their fundamental truth."

Bryan Connon
Eastbourne, Sussex

SUNLIGHT ON THE LAWN

Facsimile of the Original Edition of 1956

Morning

SUNLIGHT on the LAWN

BEVERLEY NICHOLS

With drawings by
William McLaren

JONATHAN CAPE
Thirty Bedford Square
LONDON

CONTENTS

For

R O Y N O R B U R Y

who has so often
helped to make
Merry Hall
merrier

CHAPTER I

A SHADOW PASSES

'WHAT will happen to the garden when Oldfield can't go on any longer,' I said to Gaskin, 'I really do not know.'

'You've been saying that for the last seven years,' observed Gaskin shortly. 'He'll probably walk to both our funerals.'

As Oldfield had just celebrated his eighty-second birthday, this was, I hoped, an over-statement. However, I did not argue with Gaskin. The day was hot; he had been bottling gooseberries all the afternoon; and several of the bottles had gone wrong. Instead of the clear, clean ovals of amber green fruit, which were the envy of all the ladies of Meadowstream, who always claimed that no man ought to be able to bottle gooseberries at all, these presented a sinister appearance, like exhibits in a medical museum. This had never happened before; it has never happened since; and Gaskin took it as a personal affront.

I glanced at my watch. 'If he works so hard in this heat,' I said, 'he'll be going to his own funeral before the summer's done. It's nearly ten o'clock.'

I went out to stop him. I wondered how many other employers, this evening, were walking across their lawns in the hope — probably vain — that they might be able to stop their gardeners working. Not many, surely. If Old-field had been on overtime it would have been a different matter, but he had never asked for overtime, and on the one occasion when I had suggested it, he had given me a look of such scorn that I felt as though I had insulted him.

I knew where he would be found. He would be watering the lilies. Yes — there he was in the distance, a bent black figure, plodding towards the water-tank that lay in the shadow of the old fig tree. Partly because I knew that he would resent any interruption, and partly because this was a golden moment in time, a moment to be savoured, as one savours a yellow rose, I lay down on the grass and stared up to the sky.

Oldfield, Merry Hall, the lilies — they were inseparable. The old man, the old house, and the white flowers. I should never be able to think of the one without the other, for he had been standing by the *regales* on the first magic day — seven years ago, it was — when I crept through the deserted garden, a trespasser, little realizing that this was to be my home for many happy years. It had been the sort of moment that must come to an explorer, when he has been plodding through a dark pass, and suddenly comes to a gap in the cliffs and sees, glittering before him, the snows of an uncharted mountain. I had fought my way through weeds and brambles, towards an old brick wall, had found a gap in it and there, glittering before me, were the snows of the lilies. They really *were* sunlit snow, and the fragrance, as the breeze danced over them, seemed to drift from the fields of heaven.

By them had been standing Oldfield, looking as old then as he did now. I shall always remember our first conversation. 'That's a wonderful lot of *regales* you've got there,' I had said. To which he had replied:

'Aye, they're pretty good.'

'Have they been established for long?'

'Thirty years or so.'

'Where did you get the bulbs?'

'Boolbs?' A snort. '*Boolbs?* I didn't get boolbs. I grew 'em from a handful of seed.'

'Does that take long?'

'Three years. Of course, garden book says seven. But I don't allus hold wi' garden books.'

The lilies were nearer forty years old now, except, of course, those which I had grown from seed myself. That had been one of our first jobs together, and sure enough, in three years they had flowered. Today, we had almost too many lilies. That may sound a pampered, tiresome sort of statement, but it is true. I had a great many lily-hungry friends, I had only a small, closed car, and all too many days of summer were spent crouched over the wheel of the car, while I sped round the countryside delivering them, my head reeling from their fragrance, and my neck, shoulders, sleeves and shirt-cuffs stained a deep and apparently indelible yellow from their pollen.

That was one of the reasons why I had taken to giving a party for the lilies, on the evening of the first Sunday in July. One could fill the entire house with lilies . . . lilies

dancing up the staircase, lilies crowded into every corner of
the music room, lilies piled in banks in the hall, lit by
candles in silver sconces, lilies clustered thick in the old urns
on the terrace. When the party was over the ladies could
take them all away, and depart in their motor cars looking
like a succession of Margot Fonteyns after a first night, and
I would be filled with a most satisfactory feeling of beneficence, which was not lessened by the reflection that it
would be the ladies' evening dresses, and not my suits,
that would be ruined by the lilies' golden but treacherous
dust. And I would go back to an empty room, haunted with
the fragrance of the luminous blossom, and tomorrow . . .
tomorrow I could pick some more.

The thought of tomorrow brought me back to the present.
Tomorrow was only a week to the party, and hardly any of
the lilies were yet in flower. There had been a drought for
nearly a month; they were thirsty souls, and they were
nearly ten days late. I had a sudden sense of urgency. It
would be terrible if the lilies were to let me down. I
scrambled to my feet and hurried across the lawn.

II

Oldfield had taken a moment's rest. He was standing
there, in the gathering darkness, wiping his forehead with
an old red handkerchief. By his side were two empty cans,
and the path from the tank to the lily-bed was muddy with
water that he had spilt.

'Still at it, Oldfield?'

'Aye, still at it.'

'Don't you think you've done enough for tonight?'

'You told me you wanted them lilies out for t'party.
And if they're to be out, they've got to be watered.'

He bent down to pick up the cans.

'I'll take them,' I said. He made no objection.

I took the cans and walked over to the tank. The reader may suggest that I might have done this before. I suppose I might. But gardening is not the only job that is fatiguing, and I had been at my desk, on and off, since seven o'clock in the morning.

The tank was filled from the tap every morning, so that the water could grow warm throughout the day, but it was already nearly empty. I had to bend low to scoop the water, and the cans felt very heavy when I lifted them.

I watered a clump of lilies and went back to Oldfield. It was so nearly dark that he would have to stop now, whether he liked it or not.

'Don't you think,' I said, 'that we could use the hose on them, just for once? It would save so much trouble. And if we were to put a sprinkler on the end of it . . . '

I went no further. Oldfield was Drawing Himself Up. This was a symbolic gesture, implying stern disapproval, and portending a lecture. When Oldfield Drew Himself Up, the aged body slowly straightened itself, the withered neck rose from its collar, and the one good eye stared straight ahead, boring through one, so that one felt like a small boy who has asked an impertinent question at maths. If these words give the impression that I am mocking Oldfield, that is the fault of a clumsy pen. One could not mock Oldfield. Nature still makes great gentlemen, and he was one of them.

He took a deep breath. His voice trembled ever so slightly as he spoke. 'I wouldn't use t'hose on them lilies if you was to pay me forty pounds.'

The sum, forty pounds, was deeply significant. It stretched back to a past even more remote than his own youth, to the days of Goldsmith, when a man could be 'passing rich with

13

forty pounds a year'. Oldfield had retained that standard of values. Forty pounds — a sum which will doubtless soon be regarded as a fitting weekly remuneration for the butcher's boy — to him represented a fortune.

'Not if you was to pay me forty pounds,' he repeated.

Then he began it all over again — Oldfield's celebrated lecture on the Evils of Cold Water. I knew it by heart. It opened with the geraniums in the greenhouse, and how the cans to water them must always be left overnight. This lecture usually went on almost interminably, with numerous striking examples of plants that had come to an untimely end through the use of water that had not been properly *chambré*. Tonight, however, he cut it short.

'But I reckon I've told you all that afore now,' he said, with a heavy sigh.

'Yes, Oldfield, you have.'

He took the hint and we walked back to the house together. On the way I asked him if he would like a little whisky before he went to bed. He said yes, he would. So I went in and poured it out, and I made it a very little one. When a very old man is very tired, at the end of a long day, a little whisky goes a long way.

It went a very long way on this occasion. Leaning against the door of the old conservatory, with the soft stars be-ginning to dust the sky, as though some careless goddess had been making her toilet and had scattered the floor of the night from a silver powder box, Old Oldfield began to talk of the past . . . of Merry Hall . . . of the good old days. I let him wander on; talk, with him, was a physical as well as a spiritual relaxation; it seemed to loosen his tired muscles, and to soften the wrinkles round his eyes.

'Aye,' he was saying, 'those were the times when a man wasn't ashamed of doing a day's hard work.'

14

This seemed the moment to bring his little monologue to a close.

'Well, Oldfield, you've certainly done a day's hard work today, and more. Swallow that up, and run along to bed.'

He drank his whisky, and smacked his lips. Then he handed me the glass. 'Thank you kindly, sir,' he said.

He touched his cap and turned to go. Then he paused, for there was one last thing he wanted to say. 'Aye,' he muttered, 'I've done a hard day's work. And I allus shall.' His one good eye blinked up at me. 'Because you see, sir, it's like this.'

'Yes, Oldfield?'

For a moment I was afraid that he might be about to begin again — that this was the cue for a further excursion into the past.

'It's like this, sir,' he repeated.

'Yes, Oldfield?' I hope that my voice did not sound impatient, for it was now that he was to say something which I shall never forget. Of all the homely words of wisdom which I had heard from him, in these last seven years, this was the one which I cherish most.

'I want to wear out,' he said very softly. 'To wear out. Not to rust out.'

It was not 'rust' as he pronounced the word; it was 'roost'; the gentle accent in which his thoughts were clothed.

To wear out, not to rust out, to pass on with one's old spade still bright from use . . . it was a sentiment that I well understood.

'Yes, Oldfield. I'm sure that is how it will be.'

He nodded. Then he touched his cap. 'Good night, sir.'

I heard his footsteps walking slowly, very slowly, down the little path. Then I went indoors. The house seemed strangely empty.

III

The party was a glittering success; the lilies were à *point*; and all the ladies were in ecstasies. So, I suspected, would be the local dry-cleaners, who would shortly be receiving an avalanche of curiously stained evening frocks. And since the drought had broken, and the next few weeks were cool and calm, Oldfield seemed to take a new lease of life. Perhaps Gaskin had been right after all. Perhaps he would walk to all our funerals. One thing, at least, was certain; whatever else he was doing he was not rusting. Nor 'roosting', in either sense of the word. He was keeping his spade bright.

And then, something happened which made me realize that he could not go on much longer. He had come very nearly to the end of his garden path.

It was in mid-October. To be precise, at five o'clock on October the fifteenth, when darkness was falling, when the giant poplars in the field across the lane were etched in charcoal, and when, as always, from the distant spinney, there drifted the wild, harsh music of the rooks.

I met him walking across the lawn, on his way back to tea. He looked all in. The fine features were drawn and haggard; his shoulders drooped with fatigue. I longed to say to him: 'For God's sake, Oldfield, take a day off . . . or at least put your feet up for an afternoon.' I said no such thing, for as we all know, it would have been useless, and would have been construed as an insult.

So I said something about it having been a nice day.

'Aye,' he agreed, straightening himself with an effort. 'I knew t'would be like this, way back in April.'

This seemed such an unusual example of meteorological foresight that I could not restrain an expression of surprise.

16

'Aye,' he continued, 'way back in April I said to my son, "You take your holiday in October this year," I said. "Then you'll be sure of fine weather." '

'How could you know, so far ahead?'

'Because t'oaks were budding ahead of t'ashes, of course.' There was a note of impatience in his voice, as though he were reproving me for my ignorance. He lifted his forefinger to emphasize the point. . . .

' "Ash before oak and you're in for a soak, oak before ash and you'll just get a splash." I never know that to fail, not in the last sixty years. There's a lot o' truth in them old sayings.'

'I must remember it.'

I began to perform the evasive action known as 'The Oldfield Glide,' which is necessary when a conversation with the old man has to be brought to a conclusion. This manœuvre consists in gradually edging away backwards, saying 'Yes' or 'No' or 'Really', while he continues to talk, until one is almost out of earshot, when one darts for cover. It was not because I was bored, but because I longed for him to go home and rest.

But he was not finished. He had something over his arm — a sort of sack, which he had been fingering while he was speaking, as though he wished to be rid of it and yet were loath to part with it.

'I've brought t'sack,' he began . . . and then he stopped, and I saw, to my distress, that his throat was gulping, as though he had been overcome by an overwhelming emotion. I could not imagine what was worrying him, nor what 't'sack' might be for. Had there been a tragedy? Was he going to bury something? I had no chance to ask him, for he abruptly changed the subject.

Blinking at me with his one good eye, and holding the sack behind him, he barked the single word 'Sloogs!'

This was unexpected. Whatever purpose the sack might have, it could not surely be for slugs. One does not collect slugs in sacks unless one is of an eccentricity verging on the morbid. I gathered that he was playing for time, and that the slugs had only been introduced, as it were, as a *divertissement*, to play their brief role until we were ready for the deeper and more disturbing problems of the sack. This conjecture proved to be correct.

'Never did I see such a year for sloogs,' he proclaimed. 'If Gaskin gets a stick more celery for your dinner, he'll be lucky.' (I need hardly say that we had celery as large and firm as elephants' tusks, for weeks ahead. However, that is by the way.)

The eye fixed me with a haughty reprimand. 'That stoof you bought to put on sloogs wasn't no good.'

'I'm sorry. It was supposed to be the latest thing.'

'Aye, maybe it was. But t'latest thing's usually t'worst thing, these days, in my opinion.' He shifted the sack from one arm to the other. 'Now, if we'd only had t'soot. . . . '

This was really a little unfair, and for a moment my curiosity about t'sack was forgotten by my sense of injustice about t'soot. For months t'soot had been thrown in my face. We had no t'soot of our own because I had made an alteration in the central heating plant. I had asked Oldfield, time and again, to order as much t'soot as he wanted, but he had never done so. Really good gardeners, really great gardeners, are always like that. You tell them to order things; you are quite *grand seigneur* about it, and suggest that the world is at their disposal, and that they can go up to London, if they so desire, and come back with cartloads of fertilizers, gadgets, weedkillers, and t'soot, as long as they don't bother you about it. They never do these things. They never go up to London. They lurk in their tool-sheds, brooding. And then, months later, when you congratulate them on the magnificence of the dahlias, they heave deep sighs, and explain how much better they would have been if only there had been just one barrow-load of manure, or a single sack of t'soot. It is inexplicable, it is maddening, and it is one of the many links which the great gardener has with the great prima donna.

I would have protested, but he was holding out the sack again. And there was something about the way he held it, a sort of tragic resignation, that made me realize that this was a moment of great importance to him. I held my peace.

Then he spoke again. 'It's t'sack for t'pears,' he said softly. 'The same one as I've used for forty years.' He fumbled with an object that he drew from the pocket of his apron. 'And here's t'hook that goes with it.'

I stretched out my hand to receive them from him, but he was not quite ready.

'They're not mooch,' he said, 'not in the way of gadgets, like. But they're good enoof to get t'pears.' He gave the sack a pat, and shook his head. 'That's to say, they're good enoof to get 'em, if you can see 'em. But I can't see 'em no more.' Another shake of the head. 'I was up in t'orchard this afternoon, with t'ladder. It was all a daze. All just a green daze, up in t'branches. I couldn't see 'em. Them pears is too good to waste. That's why I brought t'sack. I was going to give it to Gaskin, but seeing as you're here. . . .'

There was a rough gesture, and he thrust the sack, and the hook — a piece of crooked wire on an old stump of wood — into my hands.

He pulled himself straight and touched his cap.

'Good night, sir,' he said.

He turned, like a soldier on parade, and walked away.

I stood there, fingering the sack. It was now almost

night, and the first stars were beginning to sparkle, like far-away flowers, in the dark territories of the sky. It was very quiet, for the rooks had ceased their chorus and folded their wings. There was a touch of frost in the air. Up in the orchard the pears would be lying heavy on the branches; some of them would be dropping, tonight, into the long dank grass; there would be nobody to gather them.

I thought of Oldfield, and those pears, and the darkness was suddenly lit by a host of happy memories. I thought of those enchanted, secret moments in the old fruit room next to the tool-shed — and how I used to have to search for the key of it, which he always hid in a crevice of the wall — and how the key would not open the door unless you put it in upside down, and pushed it very hard to the left. Then you opened the door and stepped inside; for a moment there was darkness and nothing but the perfume of the pears. There was the scent of Gloire de Comice from the espaliers in the kitchen garden, and from the old arches against the south wall, and of the gnarled, twisted trees of Williams, in the orchard.

I thought of summer mornings in February, sitting at the breakfast table, cutting a pear with a silver knife, and marvelling at the sweet summer juices that dripped on to the plate. That was a miracle that never lost its freshness. Here I was, in deep winter, and if I turned my head and looked over my shoulder I should see white fields and a snow-bound world. But in front of me, on a green plate, was the sweetness of the summer; by some enchantment of nature the showers of April and the dews of June had been distilled into a magic, living casket, and had been preserved, through the long bitter winter, for my delight.

All because of Oldfield – the old scarecrow, perched up in the trees like some strange, encroaching bird. All because of the old man who had been so gruff and rude when anybody borrowed his ladder — the ancient martinet who had told us to mind our own business when we had asked if we might hold it for him, because . . . he was not so young as he used to be.

Well, it was finished now. His climbing days were done. It was 'just a green daze, up in t'branches'. And it was a sad moment, for all of us.

But it was not, essentially, a tragic moment. For I knew that he had been happy on his ladder, and that there had been many times, in his long and honourable life, when it had lifted him a little way to heaven.

IV

On the following morning, before I was up, Mrs. Oldfield came round to the back door with a message. Oldfield, she said, would not be coming to work that morning. The poor old lady had taken quite a while to say these simple words, for it was the first time she had been obliged to say them in the whole of her long life, and it must have been almost as bad for her as for him.

At first I hoped that it might be nothing serious. Perhaps, at long last, he had realized that there was a limit even to his endurance. Perhaps, after a rest, he would be able to carry on again. Then, two days later, the doctor came to see me. Oldfield was very ill indeed. He had pneumonia and pleurisy, and his heart was affected.

The question was not easy, but I had to ask it. 'Does that mean he has no chance?'

'He would have a better chance if I could persuade him to go to hospital.'

'But can't you?'

'He is a very self-willed old gentleman.'

'So I have found. But I think I know how you can

persuade him to go to hospital. Tell him that unless he goes he will never be able to work again. That is the only word that will influence him . . . work.'

The doctor looked at me curiously. 'But surely you realize that he never *will* be able to work again?'

I suppose that I had realized it, subconsciously, but to hear it put into words, by a man of authority, was almost more than I could bear.

'Not even very light work?'

'Not even that.'

It was on the tip of my tongue to ask whether he might not at least 'supervise', but I refrained. The idea of Oldfield 'supervising' a younger man was grotesque. Neither of them would endure it for five minutes. I could see the old man standing over him, boring into him with his one eye, harrying him, scolding him, seizing the spade from his hands . . . no, it would never do.

'All the same,' said the doctor, 'I will follow your suggestion. Let us hope it works. For if he doesn't go into hospital, and quickly . . . ' He finished the sentence with a shrug of the shoulders.

After the doctor had gone, I walked over to the greenhouse. There would be a great deal to do. Up till now, without wishing to claim any saintly virtues, I think I may say that I had been more concerned with Oldfield's problem than my own. His could be called a tragedy; mine could not; all the same, it was a great inconvenience. Months might pass before I got another gardener; and whatever happened, there could never be another Oldfield. In the meantime the garden had to be kept going. A garden is a living thing; you cannot shut it up like an empty room, and draw down the dust-sheets; it demands incessant attention. Who was to give it that attention? I was in my usual state of trying to finish a book which ought to have been delivered to the publishers months ago; Gaskin could not add to his responsibilities; and even if I could find an odd man, how very odd he might, and almost certainly would, turn out to be!

There was only one bright spot on the horizon; at last I should be able to turn out the tool-shed, or rather the various rooms and lofts adjoining the old stables in which Oldfield, for the past forty years, had been accumulating the paraphernalia of his craft. I had been longing to do this for seven years, but I had always been thwarted. On the few occasions when I had dared to throw anything on to the rubbish heap, he had always retrieved it, like an ancient and infuriatingly persistent spaniel from whom it is impossible to hide a favourite bone. There was, for example, an old water-sprinkling cart that we had never used; it must have dated from the beginning of the century; it was covered with rust and so cumbrous that it took up half a shed. I trundled it out and dumped it on the rubbish heap, hose and all. Next morning, when I drew up the blinds, there it was, in the middle of a scorched patch of the lawn, spouting defiantly, if somewhat spasmodically, like some weird fountain traced by the pen of Emmett.

This, and a hundred other picturesque but outworn relics, I should now be able to jettison. When the watering was finished, I walked back to the stables and opened the door — rather timidly, for even now his stern presence could be felt all around me. Facing the door, on a rusty hook, hung his ancient panama hat, and it was so familiar, and had moulded his head for so many years, that I seemed to see his face underneath it, staring at me with the one good eye. This was absurd; one could not allow oneself to be dominated by a hat; on to the rubbish heap it must go. I stretched out my hand, and took it off the nail, and was about to throw it out, when I paused. The hat suddenly seemed to acquire a symbolic quality, like a battered crown; to throw it on to the rubbish heap would be *lèse majesté*; worse, it would be an act of unkindness. I would not throw it on to the rubbish heap. I would keep it for him . . . one never knew. But I would not put it back on the hook. It stared at me too intently.

So it went into an empty cupboard, and there, for all I know, it reposes to this day.

V

And now, if you choose, you can skip till the next chapter, for nothing more is going to happen in this one except a lot of rummaging about in a succession of dusty stable rooms — which at every twist and turn evoked the ghost of an old gardener whose likeness I wish to keep fresh in my memory. How could you be interested, for instance, in the old chest which I found underneath a heap of tattered netting? I dragged it out and prised open the lid, and what do you think I found? A heap of faded Chinese lanterns! I doubt if anybody under thirty will know what is meant by Chinese lanterns. For the enlightenment of these lucky people, let it be stated that Chinese lanterns were an essential feature of all country fetes and parties when I was a small boy — though even then they were growing 'old-fashioned'. They were coloured paper lanterns with a little socket on the base for a candle; you stuck in the candle and lit it, then you pulled up the lantern, which opened up like a concertina, and you marvelled at the glow of rosy pink or soft green that greeted you. After you had lit the lanterns, you put a cord through the ring at the top of them, and strung them up in the hall, or in the room where you were going to dance. And your mother was in agony in case they should go up in flames, which they sometimes did, and the servants were rebellious because of the wax which they would have to clean up in the morning, and the little boys danced with the little girls in the pink and green shadows, and it was all a wonder and a wild desire.

How could you be interested in such things as Chinese lanterns? But I was interested in them. I could see them strung across the lawns of Merry Hall, fifty years ago, when the great copper beech was still, by comparison, a stripling, and Oldfield a young man — 'passing rich' on his forty pounds a year. I tried to open one of them, but it split and crumbled in my hands, and tiny fragments of paper fluttered on to the floor, like the petals of a rose long faded.

And now I must start skipping too, for there is a sadness about these memories, and this small volume was intended to catch the sunlight on its pages. So I will hurry past the armoury of forgotten tools, the worn-out rakes, the ancient hoes, the frail barrows; I will not open the cabinets of seeds that had never been sown; I will pass lightly over the gumboots that had long been worn out and the gardening gloves that had never been worn at all. I had given them to him on our first Christmas together, and he had received them with a natural courtesy, but I knew that I had made a mistake, for he never wore them. And the following year, when I found him with his hands deep in the clusters of a rose which he was training to the wall, he had turned to me with a kindly smile, and had said: 'I reckon some of the young 'uns would be wearing gloves for a job like this. But I don't hold wi' gloves. What I allus say is, a man don't put on gloves when he makes love to a woman. No more he should when he tends a rose.'

'If this is your idea of skipping,' the reader might protest, 'heaven help us if you ever decide to meander.' The protest would be justified. And so there will be only one more item from this gallery of memories. It is an old seed catalogue. It was lying on a high shelf, on top of a heap of ancient bills and circulars. It slid down from the heap and fell to the floor in a cloud of dust, opening itself at my feet, as though it were asking me to examine it. I picked it up and turned to the title page. It was the annual catalogue of the royal and ancient firm of James Carter and Company; the year was 1910.

I sat down on the edge of a barrow and flicked over the pages. What a tale of opulence, of spaciousness, of vanished pomps, lay in those yellowing sheets! The title page alone was like a glittering scroll, with its reproductions of the crests and quarterings of royal European dukes, and its proud announcement that the firm had been commanded so supply seeds to His Imperial Majesty the German Emperor at Park Sanssouci . . . this same German emperor who, a few years later, was to set the Oldfields of Britain on the march.

There were nearly three hundred pages to the catalogue; we were back in the days when paper shortages were unknown; and as I turned the leaves I had a feeling that this was an age when flowers grew more slowly, when petals unfolded at their leisure, and the peaches ripened later on the wall. I was struck, too, by the number of varieties that seem to have gone out of fashion; here was a treasury of forgotten flowers. How often today, for instance, does one encounter the butterfly cyclamen, with petals like frilled petticoats? Who grows, any more, those enchantingly ridiculous calceolarias, with their toad-like faces and their bewildering mixtures of yellow? And the sweet white violets and the giant mignonettes . . . where have they gone? As for the prices! You could buy a plant of lemon-scented verbena for a shilling, and hot-house fuchsias for ninepence apiece. Even 'Palms, in variety', were obtainable at three and sixpence. The idea of ordering even one palm today, let alone a 'variety', seems fantastic. This single item conjured up a vivid picture of the fabulous institution, the Edwardian greenhouse, with its lovers whispering in the shadows, and through the scented darkness the distant tinkle of a Viennese waltz.

VI

So we reach the end of a chapter — a chapter in the history of the great world, and a chapter in the history of the little world of Merry Hall.

And Oldfield? He is still with us. Very much with us. He does not work in the garden any longer, for the doctor spoke truly when he said that those days were over. But he is often to be seen, walking by my side, and if you could hear what he was saying, you would realize that he has changed very little. There are always the same prophecies of gloom. None of the seeds I have sown, he assures me, will 'coom oop'. But then . . . he always used to say that about the seeds he had sown himself. Never — whether it is spring, summer, autumn or winter — has he known such a season, for drought, or rain, or sun, or wind . . . or 'sloogs'. But then . . . he always said that too. As he plods along, peering at shrubs, groping with his fingers through the branches of a climbing rose that he planted himself, long ago . . . a rose that today sheds a crimson shadow on the roof . . . I have a feeling that Time, for him, is a flower, and that he is gently tying the tendrils of the present to the roots of the past.

Yes, Oldfield is still with us, and as long as Merry Hall stands his shadow will lie over the sunlit lawns. When the end comes, he will not need me to tell him that he has worn out, not rusted out. His spirit is of stainless steel.

CHAPTER II

GREEN FINGERS

IF you had been able to float over Meadowstream on a magic carpet you would have seen a patchwork of fields and woods, ribboned by winding lanes converging on the village green; and this patchwork would be spread between the downs to the south and the dark mass of Ladslove Hill to the west. You would also have seen, I regret to say, an advancing fringe of red brick villas, still distant, but coming near enough to spread a certain amount of alarm and despondency to the older residents. We will avert our eyes from them. They need never trouble us at Merry Hall, because we are grand enough to be surrounded by our own land, and in any case we have planted such vast quantities of evergreens that nothing short of the Empire State Building could ever cast an alien shadow over our privacy.

'What a peaceful place!' you might well say to yourself, as you peered over the edge of the magic carpet. 'How lucky are the inhabitants of this rural retreat! What spiritual calm must invest them . . . what sweet thoughts must fill their minds!' How could you be expected to guess that Meadowstream, in reality, was not a peaceful place at all? Why should you suspect that it was torn by violent emotions and riven by passionate rivalries — that its inhabitants were constantly holding their breath, awaiting the outcome of a succession of rural dramas?

Such, however, was the case. There were no less than three of these dramas, mounting to a climax, on this last summer of the Oldfield regime.

There was the drama of Our Rose, and her sudden discovery that she had powers of spiritual healing, and the awful effect that this discovery was to have on another of my neighbours, Miss Emily Kaye.

There was the drama of little Miss Mint and her monstrous tenants, the Stromens, who at this very moment were moving into her cottage, with results which not even the most pessimistic could have forecast.

And there was the drama of The Fence, which very nearly split Meadowstream into two warring camps.

With so much dangerous material, it is difficult to know where to begin. Perhaps it would be best to deal first with Our Rose and Miss Emily. These two ladies will be constantly drifting in and out of these pages, and the sparks that they so often strike from one another — and from me — will play a considerable part in illuminating our pages.

The Rose-Emily drama opens, typically enough, with a visiting card. A little slip of paste-board, deposited by female fingers on a silver tray. A gentle, delicate symbol, you would have thought, but again you would be wrong; like everything else in Meadowstream, it was potentially explosive.

Meadowstream must be one of the few villages in England where the ladies still leave visiting cards when they call — one card if the lady is single, and two cards if she is married and unaccompanied by her husband. A wealth of tradition is enshrined in this custom, such as the letters P.P.C. scribbled in the bottom left-hand corner. P.P.C. means, of course, *pour prendre congé*, and implies that the lady is about to go away on her holiday. An unnecessary warning, in most cases, since she has usually been talking of nothing else for the past six weeks.

By the older residents these cards are collected in china bowls, which are placed on the hall table for all to see. As the years go by, the pile of cards gets deeper and deeper but . . . by a curious coincidence . . . the cards of titled persons always seem to remain floating on the top, while those of humbler folk sink to the bottom, out of sight. Thus, in every such bowl you will see a card bearing the name of Lady Blane, although this lady has been for the past ten years in an institution. In some households you will also see an outsize card inscribed, in Gothic type, Princess Romanoff Romanoff. Very imposing it looks, although by now it is growing rather yellow; and only the very oldest residents remember that the Princess was, in fact, a saleswoman for refrigerators, who left Meadowstream under a cloud considerably bigger than a man's hand.

I do not keep cards myself, because most of them seem to be from gentlemen who have something to do with the gas, but I am always happy to be called upon. It was therefore with particular pleasure, one hot Sunday afternoon, that I returned from a walk in the woods to find, on a silver tray, a card bearing the inscription:

ROSE FENTON

FLOWERS

So Our Rose was back! Our unique and invariably exciting little Rose, with her mousy hair, arranged *à la Madonna*, and her large moonstone eyes and her even larger moonstone necklace, and — in spite of her general air of cushion-like softness — her remarkable capacity for creating trouble.

Even this card, so apparently innocuous, was a potential bombshell, and I hardly dared to think of the effect it would have upon my other favourite neighbour, Miss Emily Kaye. For over a year Miss Emily had been growing more and more irritated by Rose's increasing success as a floral decorator; every time she saw her photograph in the newspapers there was a minor explosion, and when, as a crowning triumph, Rose was asked to broadcast in 'Woman's Hour', she retired to bed for twenty-four hours.

And now — this card! It certainly was rather pretentious. No 'Miss' — just 'Rose Fenton', as though she were a great actress. (Which, in a sense, she was.) And the single word 'Flowers'. Implying, of course, that she was Mistress of all the Flowers of the World, who had no need to explain herself.

My thoughts were interrupted by Gaskin, who came in from the garden with a basket of blackcurrants. 'Miss Fenton's only just gone,' he said, 'but she's coming back. Miss Emily's in the water-garden. Shall I bring tea out there?'

'That would be very nice.'

I went out, still holding the card in my hand.

31

II

'So you've got one, too?' snorted Miss Emily, glancing at the card as I greeted her. 'Did you ever see anything like it?'

I murmured something non-committal; it is my role to play the part of peacemaker between these two ladies.

'Who does she think she is? The Queen of the May?'

'Perhaps it is her professional card.'

'It may be professional but that doesn't prevent it from being perfectly preposterous.'

This sentence, so heavily loaded with p's, caused Miss Emily to spit into the air, ever so slightly, and in the embarrassment caused by this unladylike lapse, tension was momentarily relieved.

We sat down, and I studied her out of the corner of my eye. She was looking remarkably well, and although her hair was lightly flecked with grey, it was difficult to believe that she was over forty. Her skin was radiant, her sharp grey eyes were very clear, and she held herself as straight as the poker which, only a few weeks before, she had cracked over the head of a burglar who had rashly assumed that all maiden ladies were defenceless. I was about to steer the conversation to this heroic episode — although it was by now a stale one — when she reverted to the attack on Our Rose.

'She grows more ridiculous every day. Do you know the latest? She talks about her Lilia!'

'Who is Lilia?'

'Not a person — the flower. Liliums. Personally, I think "liliums" is affected enough, "lilies" is good enough for me. But really — to talk about lilia! I felt like biting her.'

'Did you?'

'No. But I showed her what I thought of it all by asking

if she had any lilia of the valley. That rather damped her. But mark my word, it'll be croci soon, instead of crocuses, and rhododendra and delphinia and heaven knows what. However, there's something else . . . something really sinister. . . .'

III

We were interrupted by the arrival of Gaskin with the tea, and since Gaskin is a favourite with Miss Emily — as, indeed, with all the ladies — and since she was particularly anxious to obtain from him a recipe for vegetable marrow pickle, there ensued a brief interlude of household gossip, in which I was not obliged to take part. I was therefore able to speculate on the nature of the forthcoming revelation.

Sinister? What could Miss Emily mean? Maddening, maybe . . . flamboyant, even moonstoney . . . but sinister? And yet I had a faint inkling of what was at the back of Miss Emily's mind, for Rose, it must be admitted, had been behaving very strangely during the past few months. She had been aloof, she had given an air of preoccupation; indeed, one might almost have described her as *distraite* by some malaise of the soul, if one had not known that she was far too shrewd a business woman to allow herself to be distracted by anything but the authorities of the Inland Revenue.

It seemed fairly obvious that she was preparing a stunt of quite exceptional magnitude. (Though it would perhaps be unjust to accuse Rose of anything so vulgar as a 'stunt'; she really believes in her obsessions, which is why they are so fascinating to the onlooker.) However, she had as yet given us no clue to the nature of the revelation she was preparing; she had merely tantalized us with vague hints and shadowy allusions. Thus, on several occasions in the early spring, she had appeared at cocktail parties with a marked pallor, sinking heavily into a chair and complaining of 'exhaustion'. Miss Emily, who liked to know the reason for everything, would then ask why she was exhausted, accompanying her question with ironic suggestions that she must have been engaged in floral activities of unusual originality, such as roofing the Albert Hall with petrified hydrangea blossoms. To such facetious notions Rose's usual reply was a forced smile and a weary shake of the head, though from time to time she allowed herself to observe that she had been 'helping'.

'Helping whom?'

'Anybody, dear, who needs help.'

'Good heavens, I should have thought we all needed help nowadays. My cook. . . .'

Whereupon Rose had waved her hand in front of her face, as though she were brushing away a tiresome insect. 'Always our dear domestic Emily!'

Miss Emily bridled. 'I have not the least desire to be domestic. I detest domesticity. But somebody has to do the washing up.'

'Yes, dear. I'm sure you're right.'

In the ensuing pause you could almost have heard Miss Emily's nostrils opening and shutting, so acute was her irritation. But curiosity compelled her to keep a semblance of politeness.

'Well, it's certainly very kind of you to help in this way, whatever way it may be, particularly when you are so occupied.'

'It is not a question of kindness,' replied Rose loftily. 'It is a question of Being Used.'

'Used?'

'Yes, dear.'

'But what for?'

To my dismay, Rose had then extended her hand in my direction. 'I am sure that *he* will understand.'

Miss Emily was not to be put off by such a subterfuge. 'Is it a sort of spring-cleaning?'

Whereupon Rose had given a tinkling laugh, and had thrown me another look, to indicate that we were in some romantic conspiracy together. 'Yes!' she exclaimed. 'I think we may call it a sort of Spring Cleaning, mayn't we?'

The alarming implication was that some form of spiritual spring-cleaning was in question, and this was not a problem that I cared to discuss with Our Rose.

So I changed the subject there and then, and I had been changing it ever since.

But now, it seemed, matters were coming to a head.

IV

Gaskin departed, Miss Emily folded the pickle recipe in her bag, and we sipped our tea. It was very pleasant, sitting by the water-garden . . . a long formal pool, fringed with rushes and irises and wild spiraeas, that caught the green shadows of the liquidambers that I had planted seven years before. It was not a large pool, but if one half closed one's eyes one could transform it into an immense lake, over which one could make daring expeditions on a drifting leaf, sailing, in imagination, under tropical trees — (the bulrushes) — taking refuge in flowery jungles from the vast monsters that swept through these deep and dangerous waters — (the goldfish) — and ducking one's head against the assault of the winged monsters with which the skies were infested — (the mosquitoes).

But such adventures were impossible this afternoon. Miss Emily returned to the attack.

'Have you seen her since she came back? No? Then you're in for a shock. All that business about "helping" — all those hints about special "powers" — do you know what it all amounts to? She's become a spirit healer!'

I sat up with a start. At the risk of introducing a false note into these frivolous pages, I feel obliged to attest — before Miss Emily goes any further — my firm belief in the reality and the importance of spiritual healing.

Miss Emily must have noticed my reaction, for she went on: 'I know that you believe in that sort of thing, and I'd be the last to deny that there may be something in it. After all, everybody knows about the village fishmonger, and the way that friend of yours cured him of arthritis by absent healing, though it certainly doesn't seem to have improved the quality of his fish. But really, when it comes to people like Rose, it's just a joke.'

'Does she claim to have healed anybody yet?'

'That's the whole point. She doesn't work on people, she works on plants, which somehow seems to make it worse. Only this morning she was drifting round my herbaceous border, looking so odd that I thought she was sickening for something. Then she began to wave her fingers at my Japanese anemones, which were drooping, because they'd only just been transplanted. And when I asked her what she was doing . . .'

She stopped abruptly. 'There she is. I'll tell you later.'

In the distance I saw Our Rose walking slowly towards us, moonstones, madonna hair and all. I rose to greet her. As it is rather a large lawn we both began to put on our smiles too soon, and by the time we met we were grinning like marionettes; once one has put on a social smile, it is difficult to switch it off.

'So lovely,' she murmured, 'after all this while.' She

sank into a chair next to Miss Emily, to whom she blew an affectionate kiss. 'Such peace! Such a haven — after all my racketings about!'

I congratulated her on the success of her lecture tour, which had been the cause of her absence from Meadow-stream.

She inclined her head, in the manner of a queen receiving homage. 'Thank you,' she replied. 'Yes, I think we may say it was a success. In Manchester, we had to turn people away. Hundreds of them. And in Leeds, too.'

'Your agent should have hired larger halls,' observed Miss Emily.

'Yes, dear. I expect he would have done, if there had been any larger ones. But there were not. Such a tragedy, with so many people in need of Help.'

Here it was again, the fatal word 'Help', which had such an inflammatory effect on Miss Emily. She tapped her foot impatiently on the stone pavement. 'I suppose you have to pay tax on the takings?' she snapped.

'Tax, dear?' Rose appeared not to understand her.

'But you will probably be able to claim quite a lot of expenses.'

Rose shook her head, as though these mundane details were quite beyond her. 'I had really not thought about it. I have not your head for business.'

We were both struck dumb by this howling lie. Rose was on the way to making a small fortune out of her floral activities. By a lucky chance her taste — which was not mine — happened to coincide with that of the great majority of British women, who, quite evidently, like to see daffodils with their heads chopped off, and gladioli arranged in triangles and irises tortured into submission by wisted wires. Apart from her numerous articles in the women's magazines — (illustrated by portraits of herself, standing proudly by her 'creations', and wearing an expression similar to that of a female explorer who has slaughtered a wild beast) — and apart from the large fees which she obtained from society women who were too lazy to maltreat their own flowers, she had devised many other sources of revenue. There was the 'Rose Fenton Exclusive Flower Vase', which sold at a guinea, and suggested a Grecian urn on which the potter had inadvertently sat down before it was dry. There was the 'Rose Fenton Floral Calendar', with 'a thought for every week'. And the 'Rose Fenton Pot Pourri from an Olde Worlde Garden' . . . a sickly mess of petalled pottage done up in small sacks of mauve gauze. Very few of the purchasers were aware that the olde worlde garden from which these odours were distilled was situated in a back street in Whitechapel, where it was prepared by a firm of wholesale chemists.

And now there were these lectures, on which, as Miss Emily had unkindly suggested, she would certainly be claiming at least her fair share of expenses. To pretend that she had no head for business and that all this frenzy of activity was undertaken with the sole object of helping her fellow creatures was really a little too much.

V

There was thunder in the air, in more senses than one. The clouds were massing over the copper beech, but they were as nothing to the clouds on Miss Emily's face. It was on the tip of my tongue to propose that we should retire to the house, but I thought better of it. When ladies are determined to quarrel . . . or gentlemen, for that matter, or cats or dogs . . . it is as well that they should do so out of doors. Things are less liable to get broken.

So it began, quietly, but with a threatening undertone, that seemed to be echoed by the rising protest of the leaves in the trees around us.

Rose turned to Miss Emily. 'Have you been home since this morning, dear? No? I'm so glad. It will be more of a test.'

'More of a test of what?'

'You'll see, dear, when you go out to look at your Japanese anemones. You promise you *will* go out and look at them?'

'I shall not only go out to look at them; I shall water them.'

'There will be no need for that, dear. None at all.'

'Do you mean that it is going to rain?'

'No, dear. I do not. Nothing of the sort.'

'Then what *do* you mean?'

'I mean that they will not need watering. *Your* sort of watering.' To my dismay she appealed to me with a gesture. 'How does one explain these things?' she breathed.

Miss Emily saved me from the embarrassment of answering. 'Not need watering!' she protested. 'Considering that they've only just been transplanted. . . .'

'That is not the point, dear.'

'Then what *is* the point?'

Rose held up her hand. 'Just a moment.' She closed her eyes and threw back her head. A slow smile parted her lips. Then she gave a deep sigh. 'I am thinking of them at this moment.'

'So am I,' snapped Miss Emily.

Rose ignored her. 'They will be well again,' she murmured. 'You need not worry. They will recover.'

'I've not the faintest doubt that they'll recover.' There

39

was a note of growing exasperation in her voice. 'They're strong roots, they were lifted with plenty of earth, and they each had a can of water last night.'

Whereupon Rose observed: 'There are more kinds of Water, my dear Emily, than you would ever guess.' Her tone was lofty, and, in some curious way, parsonic; one felt that the sentence should have been phrased: 'There are more ways of salvation, my sisters, than ye wot of.'

'I haven't the faintest idea what you are talking about.'

'No, dear. I don't expect you have,' Rose nodded, with the utmost amiability, and gave Miss Emily her most radiant smile.

'And it's no use smiling at me in that superior way.'

'I was not aware of smiling in a superior way.'

'Then why were you smiling at all?'

'I was merely thinking how different we were from one another.'

'I hope we *are* different!' snapped Miss Emily.

'Oh . . . so do I!' breathed Rose. 'I do indeed!' She raised her eyes to the sky, as though imploring the heavens to save her from the awful fate of ever bearing any resemblance to Miss Emily.

For a few moments we sat there without speaking, while the wind rose around us. It was a puckish, mischievous wind, which blew from all directions at once, and caused the ladies to give sharp, reproving pats to their skirts, which seemed suddenly to be playing a rakish game of their own, quite out of keeping with their owners' characters.

Then Rose leant in my direction. 'Shall I explain?' she said. 'Yes?' Then she turned to Miss Emily. 'It is all a question of vibration, dear.'

'What is a question of vibration?'

'You — me — life itself. Do you see what I mean?'

'Not in the least. And even if I did, I fail to understand what it has all got to do with my Japanese anemone.'

'Ah! I'm glad you mentioned your little anemone.' Rose clasped her hands and nodded. 'Just the example I needed. Let me put it very simply. Your little anemone is sick. . . .'

'It is not in the least sick. . . .'

'Just a moment, dear . . . so difficult if you interrupt. Thank you.' She closed her eyes. 'It is sick because its vibrations were disturbed when you transplanted it. All its life it had been vibrating, and the earth had been vibrating in tune with it. . . .'

'How do you know?'

Rose winced at this coarse question. 'One either knows these things, or one does not. . . .'

'Well, I don't know them, for one.'

'No, dear. I don't expect you do. That doesn't surprise me at all.'

'And I don't see how you know them, either.'

'There are scientific instruments, dear. . . .'

'What sort of scientific instruments? And what do they do?'

It was perhaps lucky for Our Rose that she was saved from answering this awkward question by an exceptionally impertinent gust of wind, which tweaked Miss Emily's skirt so violently that for the moment all her energies were employed in safeguarding her modesty. From now on, her hands were clamped to her sides.

'So you see, dear,' continued Rose, who was in a superior position, because her skirt was longer, 'what your little anemone requires is not water, but a readjustment of its vibrations, and that can only come from an outside source, a human source . . . in short, from somebody like myself, who has the power of healing.'

Still clinging to her skirt, Miss Emily began to stutter: 'I have never heard such. . . .'

'No, dear, I don't expect you have, but it is never too late to learn.' Before Miss Emily could think of a retort she turned to me again: 'One has always *known* one was a healer, of course. One took it for granted. One *knew* that one could take away pain, merely by a touch of one's hands. But it was only recently that I realized that the gift of healing could be used with flowers as well as with one's fellow men. And do you know how the thought came to me? Through a simple phrase! Shall I tell you what the phrase was? Green Fingers!'

She had begun to address me as though I were a public meeting, and to emphasize her point she lifted her hand, in a most ill-timed gesture. For the poltergeist of a wind chose that moment to play on her the same prank that it had played on Miss Emily, and twitched her skirt to outrageous heights. But she was too heated to feel embarrassed; she smoothed it back with a single gesture, and clamped it down with her hands. And so, for the rest of the dialogue, the two ladies remained, with their arms rigidly nailed to their sides, like strange, Eastern idols.

'Green Fingers!' she repeated.

'Green fiddlesticks!' snapped Miss Emily. 'What a gardener wants is *muddy* fingers!'

'Always our dear materialist! Do you know what "green fingers" means? It means *fingers that vibrate in harmony with nature!*' (I was quite certain that this was a quotation from one of her lectures.) 'And if one's fingers vibrate in harmony with nature, one has at one's command a whole fount of healing!' (Yes, it was certainly part of the lecture, and I felt a great sympathy with Rose that she was obliged to deliver it with her hands held, as if by suction, to her thighs; it would have been even more effective if she had been able to make her usual fluttering gestures.)

'We do not expect any credit for this gift,' she babbled on, looking out to the darkening skies, as though she were speaking to the man at the back of the gallery. 'Oh no! All we ask is a little sympathy, a little co-operation. That is *really* necessary.' She came, with a bump, from the general to the particular. 'I am *almost* certain that dear Emily's anemone will recover.' (The look in her eye belied this sentiment, and suggested that she would have been delighted to learn that it had been blasted to the ground.) 'But I suspect that it has not been *helped* by her attitude. If there is a hostile influence standing by the bed of a sick person to whom I am sending vibrations, my task is made the harder. It is the same with flowers. If Emily were to ask me to treat some object in her greenhouse, to bring it into flower, for instance, and then if she were deliberately to go into the greenhouse, and send out hostile vibrations. . . .'

This was too much for Miss Emily. Speaking at the top of her voice, for the wind was growing fiercer every minute, she shouted: 'Do you seriously mean to tell me that if you sat down and sent thought-waves over to my greenhouse, you could bring my cactus into flower?'

Rose shouted back: 'No, dear, I do not mean to tell you anything of the sort. I doubt whether I should be able to help your cactus at all. There must be . . . how shall I say? . . . an *affinity*, yes, that is the word, between the healer and the healed, and cacti . . .' (she bellowed it in a very affected way, as though it were spelt 'kektay') . . . 'are not *me*. Not me at all. No affinity whatever. They may, of course, be *some* people . . .' (here she stared very hard at Miss Emily) . . . 'but they are not *me*. I am afraid I cannot help your cactus.'

Miss Emily could stand it no longer. By now she was

looking very like a cactus herself. 'I think,' she shouted, 'I think. . . .'

And a new and fiercer wind gave an extra force to her terrible words. . . .

'I think that you should have your head examined!'

At precisely that moment, a waiting Titan seized a hammer and smashed it across the skies with the most appalling thunder-clap I have ever heard. It was an atomic explosion, and it is still spoken of in Meadowstream with bated breath. In the minds of most residents it is linked with the chimney that was struck in the Post Office, the phenomenon of the stationmaster's trousers, which were ripped from him in a single, electric second . . . and above all, the cow with the crumpled horn. This creature was none other than Mrs. Maple's cow, in the field opposite my front door, and I do not deny that there had been many occasions in the past when I would willingly have called down lightning from the heavens to stop it mooing. When it was struck, and when its horn was so singularly incommoded, I felt sorry for it . . . until it started to moo again.

For me, however, this thunder-clap will always be linked with Miss Emily's terrible remark, and the many drastic consequences that ensued from it.

For a moment there was an uncanny silence. Then, the first hiss, hiss, hiss of the raindrops. Plomping down like damp fruit dropping from an overladen tree. And a great new rising of the wind.

Rose stood up.

Miss Emily stood up.

The wind compelled them to keep their hands clamped to their sides.

'Thank you, dear,' said Rose.

'Not at all,' said Miss Emily.

44

They did not exactly bow to each other, nor did they throw down their gloves on the terrace ... which was rapidly darkening with the raindrops. But there was a sinister suggestion of the hostile courtesies that precede a duel.

In silence we turned and walked towards the house — in silence and in great dignity too, which was really rather ridiculous considering that each raindrop was so large that it made us shudder. I do not remember much of the next three minutes, except that they were made hideous by the Titan with his drum, and the deluge on the roof of the little conservatory, and the white searing streaks of lightning.

In spite of these phenomena, the ladies took their departure, with icy, wax-work smiles, and an extraordinary unawareness of each other's presence. 'It has been so refreshing,' murmured Our Rose. 'So instructive,' hissed Miss Emily.

Into their separate cars they stepped. I stood there on the steps getting drenched, feeling extremely uncouth and incompetent, waiting to wave goodbye. Starting buttons were pressed. I need hardly say that Rose's button was the first to respond, and that she shot forward into the lane with ectoplasmic efficiency and a wave of a moonstone bracelet. Poor Miss Emily's button had to be pressed again and again, while I grinned, and began to wave, and got wetter and wetter. At last she, too, shot away, and I was able to go back to the music room, where One, Four and Five were all crouched under the sofa, wondering if the end of the world had come. I coaxed them out, one by one, and stroked them, and reassured them by a brief lecture on natural phenomena, which seemed to set their minds at rest. Within five minutes they were all curled up together in a furry mass on the sofa, emitting purrs that rivalled the thunder outside. Not for the first time I reflected that cats are very much less feline than ladies.

CHAPTER III

FOLIE DE GRANDEUR

So you see, Meadowstream is not such a peaceful place, after all. Sometimes I think that no part of the earth's surface on which Miss Emily and Our Rose were within hailing distance could ever be really peaceful.

However, this volume bears the title *Sunlight on the Lawn*, and so far there has been little sunlight and less lawn; we have been heaving sighs and listening to quarrels. Let us switch on our sunlight by the simple device of gathering a few of our friends round a sundial. That is where we happened to drift, a few days after the battle which we have just described.

The friends in question were Marius and Miss Mint. They have appeared in the previous chronicles of Meadowstream,[1] but for those readers who have not met them

---

[1] *Merry Hall* and *Laughter on the Stairs* (Jonathan Cape).

before, they can be quickly described. Marius is our local intellectual — but no, that gives a false impression; perhaps Marius is not so easily described, after all. For though, at Oxford, he took a double first in Greats, and though he has forgotten more history, ancient and modern, than most of us have ever endeavoured to learn, his erudition sits as lightly on him as the old black hat which he balances on his greying hair. As for his occupation, that cannot be described at all. The most we dare hint is that it lies in one of those shadowy corridors between the Foreign Office and the Secret Service, of which the great world knows nothing.

And Miss Mint? Well, some thirty years ago she was Marius's governess, and he always maintains that it was she who taught him everything he knows. It was to repay this debt that he helped to furnish two cottages which she had inherited in the neighbourhood. She is a timid, mousy little creature, who flushes easily; most people frighten her — as well they might, in view of her unhappy childhood. But she had found peace, at last, in Meadowstream.

II

Certainly it was peaceful enough, on this hushed October afternoon, round the sundial. Marius had only just bought it, from an old junk shop in Chelsea. It was a disc of worn grey stone, supported on the back of a kneeling cherub. Round the edge, in a delicate eighteenth-century script, ran the legend. . . .

> Not heaven itself upon the past has power
> But what has been, has been,
> And I have had my hour.

Marius ran his fingers over the lettering. He turned to Miss Mint. 'Do you think the words are appropriate?'

She hesitated for a moment, and — as always when she was asked for a decision — the little flush came into her cheeks. But she was a truthful soul. 'No, Marius,' she said gently, 'I do not. They make you sound like an elder statesman.'

He smiled. 'Dear me! Perhaps you would prefer Sydney Smith's variation of the same theme. . . .

> Serenely full, the epicure would say
> Fate cannot harm me, I have dined today.'

Miss Mint looked towards me. 'Marius is being wilful, just as he was when he was a small boy. He likes to pretend to be a cynic.'

'It is hardly cynical to be thankful for a good dinner.'

'No. But it is unfitting to offer those thanks on a sundial. A sundial — ' again she hesitated, and now the flush became a glow — 'a sundial . . . I am afraid that I am not very clever at expressing myself . . . a sundial should put one in a different mood.'

His smile softened. 'You are quite right, my dear.' He linked his arm affectionately in hers, and led her to a garden bench. 'What would you suggest? A fragment of Plato?'

She frowned in concentration. 'I cannot for the moment recall. . . .'

'Surely you remember? "Time is the moving image of Eternity." You once made me write it fifty times in the original Greek.'

She laughed . . . a very sweet sound her laughter made, too. 'So I did, when you were late for your music lesson. The moving image of Eternity. But even that is a little . . . intimidating.'

'Then what?'

48

Again she turned to me. 'Marius makes me feel so ignorant.'

'If that is so, I am paying back old scores.'

She put her hand impulsively on his. 'Forgive me. I did not really mean that. But the quotation I had in mind was so obvious. So very obvious.'

'What was it?'

' "I count only the sunlit hours." '

'I thought you would say that.'

'Do you know who wrote it?'

'No. Nor I imagine does anybody else. I seem to remember that it was discovered by Hazlitt one morning when he was wandering through the alleys of Venice. He looked up, and there it was, hanging on the wall. *Horas non numero nisi serenas.* Which makes your "sunlit" something of a mistranslation. Sunlight does not always imply serenity. As I am reminded at this moment.'

He rose slowly to his feet, a lanky, black-coated figure, and clapped his thin white hands. A startled blackbird rose chattering from the lawn and flew off into the wood. At the same time, an enormous cat emerged from the shadow of the camellia under his study window. It had an air of outraged dignity. This was Marius's grey Persian tom, whom he had entitled Byron, partly because it had a lame foot — (he had rescued it from a trap when it was a kitten) — and partly because its conduct frequently recalled the exploits of Don Juan. It regarded us for a moment with a baleful eye, and then disappeared into the house.

It was pleasant sitting here in the garden, chatting idly about sundials, and I was glad when Marius, resuming his seat, turned to me and said: 'But you have not told us what you would write on your own sundial.'

'I know one thing that I would *not* write.'

'And what is that?'

' "A garden is a lovesome thing, God wot!" '

'I am delighted to hear it. I have always considered that line to be the ugliest in the world's literature.'

'But the next three are even worse. "Rose plot. . . ." '

' "Fringed pool . . .",' murmured Miss Mint.

' "Fern'd grot",' concluded Marius. 'It is certainly very, very shocking. What would one do if one were asked by one's hostess to walk into her lovesome garden in order to examine her fern'd grot? It does not bear thinking of. So do not let us think of it. Surely you can suggest something better than that?'

I seemed to be in a perverse mood. 'I can only think of things I would not write. One of them is: "It is later than you think." If it is true, it is profoundly depressing.'

'But it is not true,' exclaimed Marius. 'It is the very reverse of truth. It is always earlier than you think, for the simple reason that the longer you live the more you have to learn.'

Miss Mint smiled — a rather melancholy smile. ' "Like our shadows",' she quoted, ' "Our wishes lengthen as our sun declines".'

Marius shook his head at her. 'And now it is you who are being perverse; to quote Young's *Night Thoughts* at a golden hour like this is the very height of perversity. I do not know what is the matter with you both.'

He lay back on the bench, and shaded his eyes from the last pale glare of the setting sun. 'But seriously,' he said, 'it is an enchanting subject for speculation. One day you should write an essay about it.' His words were addressed to me, but he was really speaking to himself. 'There should be sundials for every mood. There should be avenues of sundials, stretching into infinity. And men could walk

The Garden of
Merry Hall

down those avenues, and bend over those sundials, choosing the legends that fitted the beating of their hearts. If they were in an hour of triumph they could boast with Petruchio, "It shall be what o'clock I say it is." If they were in an hour of difficulty, beset with worries, and if they remembered their Browning, they could comfort themselves with the thought that "Time is for apes and dogs, man has for ever". If they were in a mood of depression, they could find their consolation in a single couplet: "Shadow and sun; so too our lives are made; But think how great the sun, how small the shade." '

'I think that would be the legend I should choose,' said Miss Mint. 'Who said it?'

'Again, nobody knows. But then, nobody knows who said half the wisest things in the world. There is one author who is greater than Homer and Shakespeare and all the rest of them, and his name is Anon.'

Slowly he rose to his feet and offered his arm to Miss Mint. 'But at least I know the name of the author who said the wisest thing about sundials.'

She smiled at him. 'Was his name . . . Marius?'

'No. His name was Hilaire Belloc. And he said:

I am a sundial, and I make a botch
Of what is done far better by a watch.'

III

If I had known of the strange paths down which I should be led as a result of this conversation, if I had guessed the wild adventures to which it would conduct me — and the enormous expense — I should have returned home in a mood of less serenity. As it was, I merely said to myself, 'It would be nice to have a sundial.' And having said it, I naturally thought of Mr. Crowther. Whenever anybody says to himself 'It would be nice to have a sundial' — or a grotto or a temple or a marble urn or a flight of steps or a few Italian fountains . . . (and we all say these things to ourselves, at times) . . . he thinks, inevitably, of Mr. Crowther.

I have written before of the fabulous institution of Mr. Crowther, which lies in the shadow of the great mansion of Syon House. And because Crowther's — which to me is one of the most magic spots in England — is a real place, and because people have suspicious minds, I am embarrassed by the thought that I may be accused of having a share in the business. This really *does* embarrass me. It would be awful if people believed that when Mr. Crowther sold a replica of the Arc de Triomphe to the Duchess of Windsor, to add lustre to her bathroom — which is the sort of thing that is constantly happening — it would be quite too awful if they really believed that I made a profit out of it, and if they suspected that a few days later a hooded figure knocked on my door and handed to Gaskin an enormous quantity of ten-shilling notes in a greasy envelope. I assure you that no such thing occurs — to my regret.

Apart from this, I have never had much patience with the convention that no writer should ever praise a commercial institution for fear of giving it a free advertisement. If I thought that the Ritz restaurant provided the best food in the world — which I do not — I should say so. It is as simple as that.

Therefore, with our heads held high, feeling immaculately non-commercial, we can step into the motor car and direct it to Isleworth, to Crowther's. And we can alight at the doors of a tall grey Queen Anne house, and . . . mind that you do not bump your head . . . we can push our way through a small door in the wall, and find ourselves once more in fairyland. Urns, grottoes, mantelpieces, fountains, statues, colonnades, domes, temples, all clustered in a fantastic disarray, stretching, so it seems, for miles, in the shade of the immemorial mulberry trees, and Mr. Crowther — dear, rubicund, glowing Mr. Crowther — advancing, somewhat absent-mindedly, to greet us.

IV

The key word — not a very euphonious one — is 'absent-mindedly'. Mr. Crowther had every reason to be absent-minded, for only a few moments before my arrival a huge lorry had arrived, carrying a cargo of marble gods and goddesses which had had purchased from an old house in the North of England. They had still to be unpacked, and they stared at us from the lorry with grey, sightless eyes, waving their muscular arms and heaving their rounded bosoms in a manner which must have been most disturbing to the traffic policemen on the Great North Road.

'Very choice,' said Mr. Crowther, approvingly. 'Probably made in England by Florentine workmen in the early eighteenth century. You must see them when I have grouped them round the lawn. Have you any statues in your garden, Mr. Beverley?'

'Not what you could really call statues.'

'They will come, no doubt, in time.'

I had a terrible foreboding that he was probably right. Statues *would* come, in time. For the moment, however, as I told him, I was more concerned with sundials.

'Ah yes, sundials. I have about a hundred very choice sundials. One of them is erected in the form of a Palladian temple. We will go and see it.'

He led the way, and I followed with mixed feelings. At the risk of sounding unenterprising, I had not been contemplating the purchase of a sundial in the form of a Palladian temple. However, I comforted myself with the thought that Mr. Crowther, when he shows one things, is more concerned that one should admire them than purchase them. As we walked, he embarked on a lecture about sundials, their history and their development, that would have made even Marius appear ignorant.

And then, suddenly, he paused. A group of workmen had just erected a long stone balustrade on one of the lawns. He led me over to see it.

'Now, *there's* something every garden should have, Mr. Beverley, a nice balustrade.'

It was an historic moment — a moment that was shaped by a most delicate set of circumstances. For if my mind had not already been conditioned, as it were, by the thought of a Palladian temple, I should merely have mumbled 'Yes' to Mr. Crowther's suggestion, and dismissed it from my mind.

As it was, I stopped and stared.

'There's nothing like a nice balustrade,' said Mr. Crowther, 'for setting off a garden.'

I went on staring. Was it conceivable that Mr. Crowther was right? The fact that I asked myself this question at all implied a sort of mental revolution, for until this moment — to be quite honest — I had not felt up to nice balustrades. I mean 'up' to them quite literally; it was a social question; I always associated nice balustrades — let us write N.B.s for short — I always associated N.B.s with stately homes, looming out of the mist with an immense park in the background, a mist from which at any moment there might emerge a stag, or a duke in plus fours, or something equally terrifying. N.B.s, to be properly placed, should be seen out of one's bedroom window in the extreme east wing on the rare occasions when one moves in N.B. circles. One goes upstairs to dress for dinner and one looks out and there is the N.B. — (it is the same N.B. that Gainsborough painted in the picture over the dining-room chimney-piece) — and there, sitting on it, is his lordship, talking to a man who is probably an ambassador, and they are almost certainly talking about shooting something, and they will go on talking about shooting something till half way through dinner, when somebody will remember that there is an author present, whereupon the conversation, like a large and cumbrous tank, will lumber in one's direction, and one will be asked if one has written any good books lately.

That was how I felt about N.B.s — until this historic moment. They went with lodge gates and very long drives and vistas of rhododendrons landscaped round the lake; they went with Grinling Gibbons carving and interminable draughty corridors and very old Steinway pianos on which nobody ever played, and muddy spaniels being patted by scruffy little boys from Eton, and visitors' books in which, when one signed one's name on Monday morning, one saw, with an awful shock, that the whole of the page before was bristling with royal signatures — Elizabeths and Marys and Olgas and heaven knows who else. And one wondered, when one signed one's name as small as possible, whether the butler would come in and rub it out as soon as one had gone.

Then, bless his heart, dear Mr. Crowther made that vibrant remark . . . 'There's nothing like a nice balustrade.' My social position seemed to take a great leap upwards. Why should _I_ not have a nice balustrade? There was no law against them. They were not a privilege of the Upper House. All one wanted was a garden, which I had got, and a number of gigantic men to set it up, who could be hired. And, of course, a certain amount of money. At the thought of the money, my social position began to waver again.

'Are they very expensive, Mr. Crowther? Nice balustrades?'

'Very,' said Mr. Crowther, with some satisfaction. Mr. Crowther, in spite of the fact that most of his treasures are sold at absurdly reasonable prices, always enjoys talking in princely terms. 'Now, a nice balustrade like that,' . . . waving his hand with a casual gesture towards the airy elegance of stone which confronted us . . . 'would cost you a thousand pounds.'

'Oh dear!'

'But then, of course, that is a *very* nice balustrade. Eighteenth century. Perfect condition. With the lions' heads on the end pieces. Very choice.'

'How much would a not quite so nice balustrade cost?'

He shook his head. Not quite so nice balustrades — I nearly wrote N.Q.S.N.B.s — were hardly Mr. Crowther's province. Then he remembered something. 'Tell you what. There's an old house in Hampshire, being demolished. Thornbury Park, it's called. Got quite a nice balustrade in the grounds. I was over there the other day, buying a few bits and pieces. A couple of Adam pavilions, a staircase, and a panelled ballroom. That sort of thing.' I liked Mr. Crowther's idea of bits and pieces. 'The chap there's a friend of mine. Man called Lever. Wanted to sell me the balustrade. But what would I do with it? I've got miles of balustrade already — literally miles. But he might sell it to you. That's to say, if it's not gone already.'

There was suddenly a feeling of terrible urgency in the air. 'Do you think it may have gone?'

57

'Couldn't say. They do go, nice balustrades. Best thing to do is to run over and find out.'

'Could I go today?'

He glanced at his watch. 'Let's see. You'll need to be there before five, when the men knock off. It's getting on for three already, and you've got nearly seventy miles. If you can do that in a couple of hours. . . .'

In less than a minute, with Mr. Lever's card in my pocket and a hastily scribbled map of the route stuck into the windscreen, I was speeding down the Great West Road. I had forgotten all about the sundial. There were greater adventures ahead.

V

I shall never forget that drive. It was vital that I should get to Thornbury Park before the sun set, and the sun seemed to be setting with unprecedented velocity. Have you ever raced the setting sun? It is an alarming experience. You see the red disc sinking, sinking down to the hills, and you look at your watch, and you press the accelerator, and then you sweep into the depths of a wood, and it is almost dark. Then you sweep out of the wood, and it is light again, and you take another look at your watch, and drive faster, faster. . . .

I made it, just as the red disc vanished.

Thornbury Park proved to be high romance. It was a desolate early Victorian mansion, built on the slopes of a hill that stretched down to a stagnant lake. The long drive was rutted, and filled with pools of water from a thunderstorm that I had just escaped. There were throngs of wild rhododendrons, with rabbits darting in and out of them.

Thornbury Park also proved to be low comedy. The

workmen were packing up, and nobody seemed to know anything about N.B.s. But Mr. Lever must be somewhere in the vicinity, and he understood these things, and no doubt would help me. So I ran round in circles, with the dusk growing deeper, looking for Mr. Lever. Finally I found him, in an early Victorian lavatory. Instantly Mr. Lever, who was evidently on a commission basis, tried to sell me the stained glass window of the lavatory, which he described as 'very choice'. Choice it certainly was, but not mine. Then, in the gathering darkness, he tried to sell me, in rapid succession, a Victorian central heating plant, about a hundred yards of Edwardian bookshelves, and a statue of Aphrodite in the last stages of elephantiasis.

At last he saw that I was in earnest. I knew what I wanted. A nice balustrade, and nothing but a nice balustrade.

'O.K.,' he said. His tone became subtly different. 'This way.'

He led me through a tall, echoing dining-room. Our feet crunched on the rubble that littered the parquet floor. We stepped out on to a terrace.

There, in the last dim light, I saw the N.B. My N.B. Mine from that first twilit moment. It was a single sweep of elegance; very simple, pearl grey, with the lichen growing round the slender pilasters. I remember thinking that it would be nice if the lichen survived the move to Merry Hall; it would make the balustrade feel more at home.

'Two 'undred,' barked Mr. Lever. 'And that's the last word.'

An ancient oriental ancestor stirred within me. I am the world's worst bargainer, and usually say yes to everybody who demands money. But Mr. Lever's 'last word' irked me. There is no such thing as the 'last word'. It is a phrase too tremendous to be lightly used. It suggests the ultimate echo — the final, awful Omega, and . . . the rest is silence. The 'last word' did not sound well, on the lips of Mr. Lever.

'A hundred and eighty,' I gulped. I felt rather nasty, as I did so. Bargaining about twenty pounds, in front of that lovely sweep of stone.

'O.K.,' replied Mr. Lever brightly. 'And, of course, you pay for the transport.'

VI

When I got home, I did not tell Gaskin about the N.B. It was only yesterday that he had heaved a dramatic sigh of relief at the departure of 'The Men' . . . the Men, in this case, being a number of young gentlemen who had been engaged for the past month on constructing a large brick pit for a specimen rhododendron, and in doing so had unfortunately disturbed the drains.

'What with the Men coming in and out in all weathers asking for cups of tea, my kitchen's not been fit to live in,' he complained. 'Now perhaps we shall have ome peace.'

I had the feeling that the arrival of several tons of N.B., in a succession of lorries, followed by the re-entry of the Men, might disturb this peace somewhat rudely.

Nor did I mention the N.B. to Ted, my secretary. There had been quite a number of dramatic sighs in that direction, too, and a great deal of talk about income tax, overdrafts, and 'cutting down'.

'But it is monstrous, Ted. I work like a black and I never spend money on anything but the garden. It wasn't as if I had enormous motor cars, or a yacht.'

To which Ted replied, tersely, that in view of all the money that was being poured into the garden, a yacht might be cheaper. Which was absurd.

Nor, needless to say, did I mention it to Oldfield. His condition was delicate enough, as it was, without subjecting him to any further strain.

So I decided that the subject of the N.B. would have to be introduced very tactfully. One could drop hints about having thought of purchasing a 'garden ornament'. Nothing definite, of course, just an idea. Then one could say that one *had* purchased it, and if asked why one had not brought it home in the car, one could say it was rather too heavy. Made of stone, you see. A statue? Oh no! Nothing so grand as that. Just a sort of little railing. And if Gaskin's nostrils began to twitch, sniffing the advent of more Men, one would laugh lightly at such a suggestion. No Men would be needed. Perhaps quite a small Man, for one afternoon.

Meanwhile, there were many enchanted hours to be spent prowling round the water-garden, which at the moment was surrounded by plain lawn, deciding exactly how the N.B. was to be disposed when it arrived. A note from Mr. Lever informed me that I seemed to have bought rather more of it than I had realized, nearly sixty yards to be precise, and since some of the blocks — the end-pieces — were the size of small cabin trunks, it was fairly obvious that we should need Men at least the size of very large cabin trunks to move them into place.

Moreover, since it would look absurd to have sixty yards of N.B. in one long straight line, it would have to be split into two, with steps in between, and that would mean lorry-loads of York stone, and terracing, and Men galore. It was all quite terrifying; it was also all quite adorable; and for days I continued to prowl round in circles, pacing out the boundaries of the imaginary N.B., walking down phantom flights of steps, and dreaming of all the lovely flowers with which the N.B. would eventually be garlanded — the white wisterias, and the scarlet-leaved vines and the yellow roses — all nodding and smiling against the grey elegance of the stone.

Yes, those were magic days. Although the N.B. was still eighty miles away, waiting to be transported in a fleet of lorries that would probably disrupt the entire traffic to the south coast, it loomed in my imagination so vividly that I could almost see it in position.

How had one supported life, all these years, without a N.B.? How indeed? One must be pretty tough, carrying on like that, with a brave smile, and not even the shadow of a N.B.

But when the telegram arrived from Mr. Lever, announcing that the N.B. was on its way, I was not so tough.

Fortunately it came when Gaskin was shopping in the village. I opened it and read: BALUSTRADE BEING DISPATCHED THIS AFTERNOON PER FOUR LORRIES STOP YOU WILL NEED ASSISTANCE. LEVER.

This seemed an understatement. Four lorries full of sixty yards of solid rock would obviously need a great deal of assistance and one could only hope that the Men in charge of the lorries would be of the Health and Strength variety. Only too often, when anything heavy arrived at the house, it was in the charge of a midget, and a very petulant midget at that, who tipped it on to the steps and vanished, hissing.

The whole thing was too alarming to be faced. Gaskin must deal with it. It was a major crisis and would bring out his best qualities. I took a piece of paper and scribbled: 'Called to London. Not back till after dinner. Some stonework will be arriving from Hampshire this afternoon. Perhaps you might get hold of Mr. Young's men to help unload it. B. N.' I read it over and wondered whether I ought to have written 'balustrade', quite openly. No. 'Stone-work' was better. It might mean anything. Perhaps I ought also to have suggested that Gaskin should put 'Five' in the linen-cupboard till the Men had gone. But that would only alarm him, and 'Five' would probably retire to the linen-cupboard in any case; he always did, when the Men were about.

I heard Gaskin's footstep in the kitchen. There was no time to lose. I seized a hat and tiptoed out through the conservatory.

The rest of the day passed in something of a daze. I did not go to London; instead I turned south, to the silence and magic of Ladslove Hill, which seemed, in the autumn mist, to be mysteriously wreathed in N.B.s. Afterwards I had tea in a village whose name I forget, and a game of darts with the landlord. Somewhere around six I dropped in to a small local cinema, arriving in the middle of a very ancient film, made in Hollywood, about high life in English society. The film, by a happy chance, was full of N.B.s, some of them the size of Stonehenge. Gaskin should see it. He could not possibly complain about my N.B. after seeing these towering erections. Moreover, these American N.B.s were the background to a story of the greatest distinction, full of duchesses who were really gangsters' molls, and titled huntsmen who rode to hounds in tights, with sawn-off shot-guns in their hip-pockets, and other typical examples of society in the shires. If Gaskin saw this film, he would see that N.B.s were quite the thing.

It was too late to have dinner, when I came out of the cinema, but it was not too late to have a drink. I needed it.

I drove home slowly, almost dreading to come to the end of the journey. I approached the house from the side furthest from the drive; I wanted to keep my first vision of the N.B., as it were, immaculate. It would have been nice to tiptoe out on to the lawn and see it before encountering Gaskin, but he was waiting in the hall. He looked extremely stern. He took off my overcoat, and hung it up without a word.

'Is anything wrong, Gaskin?'

'Oh no, sir. Nothing.' He pursed his lips and achieved a frosty smile. 'The whole place has been swarming with police, that's all.'

Police? My heart sank. Had N.B.s suddenly been made illegal? It was more than possible, with the peculiar things that were going on, at that period, in the name of British justice.

'Police? What have the police got to do with it?'

'One of the lorries broke down in the lane, and nothing could get by for three hours. It wouldn't have been so bad if half the stones hadn't fallen out of another lorry, so that Mrs. Maples's car was blocked, and she missed her train.'

'Was that why the police came in?'

'Oh no. They just had to deal with the traffic block, that's all. There was one time when it stretched half way to the post office. The sergeant said something about causing an obstruction.'

'*I* haven't caused any obstruction. Is everything cleared up now?'

'I wouldn't exactly say *that*. Both the gates into the drive have been smashed to bits. Just a heap of rubble they are.'

I could think of no comment on this disaster.

'What's more,' continued Gaskin relentlessly, ' "Five's" been missing since three o'clock.'

'He's not in the linen-cupboard?'

'He was, but he flew out when I went up to get the bandages.'

'Bandages?' One must keep calm. 'What for?'

'One of Mr. Young's men got a very nasty place on his leg when a piece of stone fell on it. A very nasty place indeed. He said he hoped you were insured.'

That sounded sinister. Was I insured? Almost certainly not. One is never insured when one ought to be. However, Mr. Young's man must wait.

'I'm sure "Five" will be back soon.'

'Let's hope so. You know what he is, with the Men about.'

'Well, they won't be here for long.'

To this outrageous observation Gaskin made no reply, and after asking — with a distinct note of irony — if there was anything more I needed, he retired.

Now for the N.B.

I walked through the conservatory, opened the door, and stepped on to the lawn. The night was very still, and there was only a thin silver candle of a moon, just beginning to emerge from under the cloak of a black cloud. For a moment I could see nothing. And then, as the cloak of the cloud fell back, and the silver wick of the moon shed its gentle light over the universe, I saw it. I saw the N.B.

And whether it was fear or delight or sheer bewilderment that filled my heart in that unforgettable second, I do not know. For there, disposed round the little water garden, was a very plausible reproduction of the ruins of Pompeii. It was a mountain of moonlit stone. It seemed to tower to the skies and to cover the whole of the garden with a tumbled ruin of masonry. It looked as though there had been an earthquake, or one of those disturbances of Nature which insurance companies describe as an act of God. (Why do insurance companies, when they want to describe an act of God, invariably pick on something which sounds much more like an act of the Devil? One would think that God was exclusively concerned in making hurricanes, smallpox, thunderbolts and dry rot. They seem to forget that He also manufactures rainbows, apple-blossom and Siamese kittens. However, that is, perhaps, a diversion.)

Earthquake or no earthquake, the N.B. welcomed me. If this avalanche of rock could have spoken it would have assured me that it was well content with the place in which it had fallen. How it was ever to be reassembled was a problem which, for the time being, I did not attempt to solve. Even in this dim light it was obvious that the Men had tumbled it on to the lawn with a total lack of dis-crimination; small pilasters were piled on top of big ones, the stones for the top railing were higgledy-piggledy with the foundations, and some of the end pieces were broken . . . indeed, a great deal of it seemed to have been smashed to bits. It did not matter. Somehow or other, in the long winter that lay ahead, it would be reassembled. Men would be summoned from the corners of the earth, and more Men, and still more Men. One must be ruthless in the cause of Beauty. One might even, with some assistance, move a small piece oneself.

I turned to go back to the house. And then, on the top of a towering mass of masonry, I saw a shadow moving. I stopped and stared. The shadow moved again — emerged into the moonlight. It was 'Five'.

This made the moment quite perfect. The thought of 'Five', fleeing from the Men, far into the night, away from his beloved linen-cupboard, had been the one blot on an other-wise perfect interlude of existence. Now he was back again. All was well. God was in His heaven, 'Five' was — almost — in his linen-cupboard, and all was right with the world.

'Five', very delicately, paw by paw, descended the impromptu staircase. From time to time he made a pleasant treble sound in his throat — a sort of 'Prrrp' — and as he did so he rubbed his cheek against a pillar, and rolled his green eyes, which caught the light of the moon. Paw by paw he came towards me, grey and white fur over grey and white stone, nearer and nearer. There was a final cheek-rubbing, and a sudden inexplicable dab at a broken pilaster, just to show that he was not going to stand any nonsense, and then, with a single leap, he was on my shoulder.

He purred all the way across the lawn. He purred as I tiptoed upstairs. (I tiptoed because Gaskin had gone to bed, and this was no moment for a resumption of our dialogue; Gaskin would certainly have got the better of it.) He purred as I lifted him up to the top shelf, and disposed him upon his favourite blanket, which was of exceptional softness and thickness, and dyed pink, with silk ribbons on the edges. How this blanket ever got into the house nobody seems to know, and in theory it is reserved for the weekend when Doris Day comes to stay. As I am unacquainted with Miss Day, and as this delight seems therefore remote, the blanket, in practice, belongs to 'Five'.

He went on purring as I gave him a final stroke, and turned out the light.

I went to bed feeling very happy indeed. 'Five' approved of the N.B., Gaskin, if properly approached, could be induced to approve of it. As for myself, I adored it. True, as yet it did not even exist. It was just a mad shambles of rock, tumbled out there in the moonlight, getting the dew on it. But as I slowly drifted into sleep, it seemed to take shape, and assemble itself, and gather itself into a single sweep of elegance. And the roses were climbing over it, and the jasmine, and the white wisteria. . . .

CHAPTER IV

SURPRISES

IT was a rough winter, both indoors and out. Oldfield had gone, and although he was succeeded by a number of quite energetic persons, male and female, the garden began to show the loss of his magic touch. Nor was its appearance improved by the fact that the contents of a small quarry were still scattered all over the lawn. There seemed to be a strange shortage of Men willing to put it together, in spite of all the advertisements that I put in the local paper. (It is extremely difficult, by the way, to frame an advertisement soliciting the services of Men to erect balustrades. However hard you try, you end by producing something that sounds like Communist propaganda.)

Perhaps it was because of the unsuitability of these advertisements that only three men appeared in answer to them, and they were quite small ones, with drooping moustaches; they took one startled glance at the quarry, paled, and vanished. It seemed as though it would stay there for ever. Well, if it did, one would have to adapt oneself to it. One would have to feign an interest in Roman ruins, and sit down to work in a classical toga.

However, 'time and the hour run through the roughest

day', and in due course the balustrade was erected, and very, very beautiful it was. And one day, into the garden walked a young man called Mr. Page, and as soon as I saw him take up Oldfield's spade, I heaved a sigh of relief. Something told me that this bright symbol had fallen into the right hands. Not that Page bears the faintest resemblance to Oldfield. He is of a different world. He is modern and streamlined; he goes to work with a sort of natural elegance, and he has enough knowledge to lecture to the Royal Horticultural Society. I hope that one day he may do so.

So spring came, and the garden smiled again, and the sun shone bright on a smoothly shaven lawn.

But there were some dark clouds racing across the sky towards me.

II

You remember Miss Mint? We met her round the sundial, with Marius, and it was he who reproved her for quoting the melancholy phrase . . .

> Like our shadows
> Our wishes lengthen as our sun declines.

Certainly this was not true of herself. Her wishes — if we are speaking of worldly wishes — had never been great. Most of her life had been lived in fear, in the dark shadow of a father who was a drunkard — often a violent one. Even after his death that fear persisted. I think that this is the case with all children of drunkards. They are beset with fears. All their memories are poisoned by a dark shape reeling by their sides . . . staggering after them down the corridors, groping towards them down the staircase. Life is not easy for the children of drunkards. In a rare moment of self-revelation Miss Mint once said to me: 'Even to this day I cannot open a closed door without a little sinking of the heart. I dread what I may see on the other side.'

However, Miss Mint had found peace at Meadowstream — as much peace as she was ever likely to find. After the death of her father she had inherited a tiny legacy, together with two small cottages. They were situated on the further side of Marius's wood. She lived in one of them; the other she proposed to let furnished. It was about this proposition that she now wrote to me.

Although her letter was typed, I knew that it came from Miss Mint, because of the mystic letters 'N.W.H.' on the envelope.[1] I opened it and read:

Beechnut Cottage

Dear Mr. Nichols,

If you are not engaged tomorrow afternoon, I wonder if you would care to have tea with me at five o'clock? I have a little Surprise which might amuse you.

I would also be very much obliged for your advice on one or two matters concerning Oakapple Cottage, which I have been fortunate enough to let.

Yours sincerely,

JENNIFER MINT

Needless to say, I should have accepted this invitation in any case, but the fact that it included a Surprise made me look forward to tea with impatience. When Miss Mint promised a Surprise with a capital S there was always

[1] For the benefit of those who are making their first visit to Meadowstream and its residents, it should be explained that 'N.W.H.' means 'Nothing Wrong Here'. This is intended to reassure the recipient that the letter contains no bad tidings. The psychologist might see in them a further example of the legacy of fear. However, we are now so used to them that they no longer suggest an unhappy symbol; they are merely a charming eccentricity, and even Miss Mint persuades herself to smile at them.

something delightful in store. Her last Surprise, for instance, to which a number of local ladies had been invited, was a lavender fan for each guest. These are the most elegant little objects, which afford fragrant refreshment during the summer months. Later on I will tell you how to make them, but they must wait for the moment, as I am already committed to a considerable diversion in our story — if it can be called a story.

You see, I want you to know Miss Mint very well. I think she is worth knowing, for there are not many people like her today. And I believe that the best way you can understand her — and what she means to me — is by coming to tea with her, and seeing the Surprise.

She is waiting for us, as always, at the garden gate, a small figure in a grey dress with a black shawl. This waiting at the gate, by the way, is another of her characteristics; when you go to tea with Miss Mint you never have to use the door-knocker; she has always been watching at the window for your arrival and pops out to welcome you. And there again — at the risk of sounding melancholy — is another legacy of the past. When she was a girl she had often to keep vigil at the window of her father's house, to be ready for the casual stranger who might enter unawares, before she had time to close the door on the dark shadow. But I must not harp on the past; it will make you think that Miss Mint is a forlorn and tedious creature, better avoided than encountered. She is not really at all like that.

So let us link our arm in hers, and walk up a path bordered with jonquils and polyanthus, and step into her tiny hall.

'Would you like tea first, or the Surprise?' said Miss Mint.

'The Surprise, please.'

'It may take you several minutes,' she warned me. Then she gave an apologetic smile. 'At least, it will take you several minutes if you like it. And I *hope* you may like it.'

'I am quite certain that I shall like it. Is it something to eat?'

'No. It is not anything to eat.'

'Something to wear? Something to smell?'

She shook her head and laughed. 'No. Nothing to smell. At least, not essentially. It is only something to look at.'

'Please show me. This suspense is unbearable.'

She opened the door to the parlour, which was even smaller than the hall. The old velvet curtains had been drawn against the sun, and the room was in shadows . . . shadows scented with the lavender and rosemary and verbena of the bowls of pot-pourri which were placed on the brightly polished tables. In the furthest corner stood her nursery screen — the prettiest thing you could desire, decorated with hundreds of silhouettes from Victorian children's books. I noticed that it had been drawn slightly to one side.

'Is it behind the screen . . . the Surprise?'

'Yes. But you must wait till I light the candles.'

She drew a box of matches from the pocket of her skirt. I could write a chapter — (do not be alarmed, I shall not) — about Miss Mint striking a match. In her fingers a match becomes a strange, explosive weapon, which flares and thunders; it seems to be invested with powers of destruction which had not previously occurred to me.

She struck the match and she lit four candles. For a few moments they flickered sulkily, then they collected themselves and became four silver flowers of flame.

She walked over to the screen and folded back one of the flaps.

And there, standing against the wall on a low Victorian table, was her 'Surprise'.

It was a doll's house, of nine rooms, which glowed softly in the light of the candles. In each room, on a tiny table or against a mirror the size of a silver sixpence, there was a little vase. None of the vases was bigger than a thimble. *But every one was filled with flowers.*

III

I looked round. Miss Mint had left the room, and I was glad that she had done so. It was a moment when it was better to be alone. I don't think that even Miss Mint would have realized quite how much it meant to me.

Here was a tiny world of its own, caught in a moment of eternal twilight, where one could enter and rest and be at peace. Sometimes I think that humanity is divided into two classes, the Shrinkers and the non-Shrinkers. If you are a Shrinker, you are able to diminish yourself at will, and to slip into the kingdom of Lilliput, not in the role of Gulliver, but as an equal. If you are a non-Shrinker, you have not this capacity and — in all probability — you have no desire for it. The test case would be a rock garden. Shrinkers, in rock gardens, are able to hide in clusters of aubretia, and conceal themselves under branches of maidenhair fern. In imagination they can scale great boulders, and climb a tree of London Pride, swinging from branch to feathery branch. There are drawbacks to being a Shrinker, of course. There is always the danger of being stunned by a dewdrop, and in wet weather one is apt to sink too deeply into the moss. After an ascent of three feet one is inclined to be out of breath; and it is a bore having to climb on to a cliff in order to look into the dreaming blue heart of a gentian. But on the whole, I think, the Shrinkers have the best of both worlds. At least, they are not obliged to bow the knee to the fashionable gods of Bigness. And they know that even if the Lord's Prayer is written on a sixpence, its message still circles the globe.

Certainly, on this occasion, confronted by this wonderful doll's house, I was thankful that I was a practised shrinker, because in a very few moments I had shrunk enough to step inside, and set foot in the hall. An elegant staircase stretched up to the floor above, and I noticed that its balustrade was made of match-sticks, painted white. At the foot of the staircase was a massive Tudor chest, made from a matchbox stained brown, and on the chest stood an immense silver salt-cellar, nearly two inches across, filled with an imposing collection of green boughs and branches. It occurred to me that so small a person as Miss Mint must have found it difficult to arrange such heavy objects. Closer inspection showed that the bunch was composed of blades of grass and tendrils of moss and fragments of maidenhair fern. There was only one flower in it — an opulent, golden blossom that suggested a tropical ancestry. It was a single blossom of polyanthus, and it was quite as large as a sequin.

The house was very still. I tiptoed up the staircase, pausing to admire the many valuable pictures that hung from the walls. The non-Shrinkers would deny that such pictures had any value; they would point out that they were, in fact, only postage-stamps, varnished and framed in silver wire. So, perhaps, they would be, in the cold light of day, outside the doll's house. But we are not non-Shrinkers, we are Shrinkers; we are not outside, we are actually walking up the staircase, and the curtains are drawn and there is eternal twilight. In such a light the pictures are very beautiful. Most of those on the staircase are of tropical scenes, showing the rugged mountains, the giant palms and the scarlet-feathered birds of Guatemala and Nicaragua. Those on the landing above are more sombre; they portray haughty royalties and stern prime ministers.

In such a setting, the bunch which Miss Mint has arranged — in a silver thimble — glows all the more vividly. It stood on a towering pedestal, fashioned from a pencil. (I wondered who had helped her to move these great pieces?) Its centre was a miniature daffodil from her rockery, peering from a little cluster made of the tips of spring grasses. Next to it was a lily-of-the-valley bell — just one bell, tinkling its floral music at the end of a slender stalk. Then there were some infant scillas, whose innocent blue shone all the more brightly because they were set against the pale folds of copper beech leaves, just as they were beginning to open. She had trimmed these leaves, with a pair of nail scissors, into the shape of tiny pink fans. (The first tints of a copper beech, before the sun tans the leaves, are as delicate as a wild rose.) There were several single blossoms of geraniums; there was the bud of a daisy; there was a sprig of lemon verbena from her conservatory, which gave to the whole bunch a ghostly fragrance . . . and I am sure that there were a great many other delights which I have forgotten. A big man could have closed his fist over the whole lot, and no doubt there are many big men who would have found pleasure in doing so.

By now I had shrunk so small that it seemed quite a long walk down the corridor, which was a good twenty inches long. I pushed open the door at the end, and found myself in what was evidently the drawing-room. For a moment I paused on the threshold, for I was no longer alone; in front of a fire of scarlet tinsel a lady was sitting, a very beautiful lady in a dress of striped yellow satin. She was perhaps rather large for my taste; in her stockinged feet she would have stood not less than three and a half inches; however, her features were so delicate and her golden hair so abundant that I could not resist an exclamation of delight.

Fortunately, the lady appeared to be sound asleep, so that I was able to examine the room at my leisure, and a most graceful room it was, in the Regency style. A striped paper covered the walls. (Miss Mint told me afterwards that she had made it from her own note-paper, ruling the stripes with a mapping pen dipped in gold ink.) The carpet was of needlework, nearly nine inches square, and embroidered with a daring design of multi-coloured roses, as large as fragments of confetti.

But it was the flowers that captivated me . . . and one bunch in particular, of quite exceptional beauty. It stood in the centre of the room, on a low circular table which, at first sight, I took to be of silver gesso. Closer inspection revealed that it was, in fact, made from an old-fashioned five-shilling piece, mounted on a tripod of silver wire. On this charming object stood a white shell, from which there rose a medley of white flowers and grasses, as delicate as a fountain of spray. In the centre were several feathery blades of pampas grass, which emerged from a cluster of white geranium buds. There were sprigs of white thorn, and some primroses . . . so pale that they were almost white. There were single blossoms of white heather, sprouting from a bed of silver lichen — the sort of lichen that one finds on fallen branches in deep woods; it is the colour of moonlight, and I have no doubt that it is greatly in demand among the more artistic circles of elfin society, for purposes of decoration. Finally, there were some airy wisps of the silver seed-pods of the wild clematis — country children call it Old Man's Beard — which she had plucked last autumn, and put away in an old chest between sheets of tissue paper. As I bent over it there was a faint scent of lavender.

It was adorable. It was more than that. As I stood there . . . shrunk, remember, to the correct proportions . . . I felt that it was also supremely important. It was a whole world of beauty on a five-shilling piece. It was a bunch of miracles that you could have worn in your button-hole. Great love had gone to its making, and great vision — the vision which enables an old lady to see the world in a grain of sand, and heaven in a wild flower. Above all, it had been composed with the supreme quality of gentleness; the frail white blossoms had been caressed into their places, the moss and the grasses had been disposed with a touch as soft as a snowflake.

Indeed, to me it was a symbol of all that is most blessed in the world.

Then the door opened, Miss Mint came back, and I had to unshrink.

Unshrinking — as all Shrinkers will agree — is extremely painful, if done too quickly. (It may also be dangerous, though of that we have no conclusive evidence.) In any case, it is always humiliating. One is suddenly faced with the fact that instead of being a sensible creature, two inches high, who can retreat into mouse-holes and sleep in Canterbury bells . . . in short, a compact and co-ordinated member of a civilized society . . . one is a gangling giant, six feet tall, with a head the size of a football, and fingers like bunches of bananas, which will never . . . no, never . . . be delicate enough to manipulate the waterfall cadenzas in Chopin's Third Scherzo. Perhaps one might not be able to manage the waterfalls even if one *were* two inches high, but one could at least bounce about on the right notes, leaping from sharp to treble, evoking agreeable echoes. Also, if one were a two-incher, one would arouse the permanent interest of cats who, when one is six feet tall, are often apt to be aloof. One would never be at a loss for feline society.

So it was several moments before I could see Miss Mint clearly, and make sense again.

'Do you like my little house?' she said.

I wish that you could have heard her voice, as she spoke, because you would have detected in it an echo that gives rather more depth to this little sentimental story. You see, there was fear in it.

And now we can go on with our story.

IV

Miss Mint walked over to the window, drew the curtains, and looked out into the garden. She seemed to have momentarily forgotten the doll's house.

'They should be back by now,' she murmured. 'They are usually here at about this time.' Then she turned round with a nervous little smile. 'I was speaking of my new tenants.'

I joined her at the window. 'Have they moved in yet?'

'I am not quite sure.' She pressed nearer to the glass. The thatched roof of Oakapple Cottage rose above the hawthorn hedge at the end of her garden, about fifty yards away. There was a gleam on the latticed panes that might have been sunlight or might have come from a light inside.

Fear is infectious; I suddenly felt a chill in the air.

'But surely you must know whether they have moved in?'

'They are rather mysterious.'

This was terrible. I had visions of Oakapple Cottage as a haunt of smugglers or spies. It was fortunate that at this moment Miss Mint remembered tea. She led the way into

the other room, where a silver kettle was steaming cheerfully on a *papier mâché* table.

'Now Miss Mint. Tell me all about it. Who *are* these
new tenants of yours?'

'Their name is Stromen. Mr. and Mrs. Stromen.'

'Young? Old? Middle-aged?'

'Quite young. And really . . . very agreeable.'

'Then why are you frightened of them?'

'I did not say I was frightened of them.'

'But you obviously are. What sort of people are they? I
mean . . . is Stromen a gentleman?'

She allowed herself a timid smile. 'I have old-fashioned
ideas of a gentleman.'

'I see. But they aren't working-class people?'

'Oh no. She is very smartly dressed. So is Mr. Stromen.'

'What does he do?'

'I gathered that he is some sort of a . . . a vocalist.'

'Oh dear! Does that mean a crooner?'

Miss Mint shook her head. 'I really could not say.' Then
she added, in somewhat brighter tones, 'His wife assured me
that he had sung on the wireless. And they would hardly
employ anybody undesirable.'

'How did they hear about your cottage?'

'They told me it was through a friend.'

'Who?'

'They did not say. And I did not press them, because I
gathered that they had been through a very trying time.
Mr. Stromen hinted that there had been some opposition to
their marriage. And Mrs. Stromen told me that her mother
had been ill.'

It all sounded rather vague and unsatisfactory, and it
seemed a pity that Miss Mint should have placed herself in
such close contact with a couple who might prove uncon-

genial. However, there was nothing in her account that could be described as actually sinister. One must hope for the best.

'I expect it will turn out all right,' I said, as cheerfully as I could manage. 'I suppose their references were quite satisfactory?'

She hesitated for a moment. 'It did not seem necessary to ask for references.'

'Oh, Miss Mint!'

'They *offered* them,' she said hastily. 'But I said that it was of no consequence. I suppose it is foolish of me, but I always feel there is something discourteous about demanding references. Besides, they both looked so very tired.'

'I can't see what their being tired has to do with not giving you a reference.'

'They didn't demand a reference from *me*.'

'I should hope not, indeed.'

'I do not think I have been entirely unbusiness-like,' she said — and in her tone there was the faintest hint of protest. 'I suggested that they might care to pay a week's rent in advance, and they agreed *immediately*. There was no hesitation *whatever*.' From the emphasis she put on these words, you would have thought that she was boasting of the part she had taken in a smash and grab raid.

'Naturally there was no hesitation,' I retorted. 'A week in advance! You ought to have demanded three months.'

She twisted her fingers nervously. 'They have a very expensive-looking car,' she murmured.

'That may be . . . but for all you know, they may be a pair of crooks.' She flinched. Suddenly I felt like a brute. Here was I, spreading alarm and despondency, putting all sorts of frightening ideas into Miss Mint's head . . . for why? Simply because her tenants had not given her a reference.

It was unpardonable of me. There had been enough fear in her life without adding to it. But my protest had been due to her very vulnerability; she was so frail and defenceless, in her tiny cottage, living on her tiny income. There was only one thing that was not tiny about Miss Mint, and that was her heart.

I forced a smile. 'I was only joking. For all we know they may be charming. And if anything happens — which it won't — you can send for Marius and me, and we'll come round and destroy them.'

Before I said goodbye we went to pay a return visit to the doll's house. There it stood, with its nine tiny rooms and their Lilliputian bouquets all glowing and sparkling in the light of the candles. The match-box staircase opened its arms in welcome, the postage-stamp portraits smiled from the walls, the three-inch lady of quality slept in front of her mimic fire. All that was lacking was a fat cat, the size of a pea; perhaps I would be able to find her one, one day. In the meantime I wished that there were some magic spell that would enable Miss Mint to shrink to the size of the sleeping lady, and enter her doll's house and live in peace. Indeed, I wished I knew such a spell myself.

CHAPTER V

ENTER THE VILLAIN

As Miss Mint had promised to call upon me in the event of any emergency, I did not do anything further about the Stromens for the moment. She was such a susceptible little creature that if I had suddenly taken to calling on her, on unexpected occasions, she might have suspected that her new neighbours were indeed a menace, and that she was in real danger. So I let matters drift.

However, rumours began to circulate, and they were hardly reassuring. It seemed that there was something 'not quite right' about the Stromens, something 'fishy' . . . so, at least, a lady at the greengrocer's said to the village window-cleaner, who repeated it to Gaskin, who passed it on to me. I could not quite gather in what this 'fishiness' consisted, but it was obviously apparent to those with a nose for such qualities. To be 'fishy', in the English countryside, is the unforgivable sin — except, of course, for authors, of whom it is expected.

My own first sight of them was not encouraging. It was at a little inn in the village, and the landlord told me who they were. Mr. Stromen had the sort of flashy good looks which one associates with a villain in a Victorian melodrama, except that instead of being dark he was very fair. His shirt-cuffs protruded too far from his sleeves, and were decorated by enamel links fashioned in the shape of bulldogs. I had sometimes seen such links in shop windows, but had naturally hurried past them, with averted eyes. It was disturbing to see them actually in use, on a human being.

Mrs. Stromen, one felt, was an ideal mate for such a person. She was also tall, and had been bleached to match her husband. She had a spurious smartness, but nothing about her looked quite clean. Her nails were very long and she was evidently proud of them and displayed them prominently. They were painted with that type of varnish which is supposed to simulate mother-of-pearl; in her case the illusion was incomplete; it suggested that she had been making shrimp sandwiches and had omitted to wash. How two such people had managed to impose themselves upon Miss Mint was beyond comprehension.

It was Gaskin, a few days later, who brought back the first eye-witness report. The Stromens, it seemed, had informed Miss Mint that they would like to make a few alterations in the furnishings of the cottage, and had asked her if she would move out some of her own very pretty bits and pieces to make room for their ultra-modern chromium plated cocktail-cabinet-cum-radio. (The thought of such an object in a Tudor cottage was in itself repulsive.) Miss Mint, needless to say, agreed, at considerable incon-venience to herself, for she had really nowhere to store anything. Gaskin, who always had a soft spot in his heart for Miss Mint, went over on his bicycle to help in the move.

When he returned, he looked grim. I went out to the kitchen to hear his report. He was sitting with 'One' on his lap, putting ointment on that wicked creature's ears, which, as usual, had been bitten overnight.

'Did you see the Stromens, Gaskin?'

'I certainly did.'

'What did you make of them?'

'Not at all the sort of people that *you* should know, sir.'

'So I suspected. But was there anything particular that made you feel that?'

'There was.' He hesitated for a moment, as though seeking for words to describe the enormity of their offence. Then, still dabbing One's ears, he went on: 'When I first met Mrs. Stromen, I naturally called her "madam".'

'That was nice and polite.'

'From my point of view,' corrected Gaskin loftily, 'it was a question of maintaining a proper distance. There were signs of familiarity, which I resented.'

'Of course. So what did she say?'

'*She* didn't say anything. It was he who said it.'

'What did *he* say then?'

Gaskin put down One, and wiped his fingers. The suspense was almost unendurable.

'He said: "Don't call her madam, Gaskin. Nobody calls her Madam. Her name's Priscilla, but everybody calls her Pris. You call her Pris, too." '

'Good heavens! Whatever did you do?'

He folded his arms and looked me straight in the eye.

'I *called* her Pris,' he said.

It must be admitted that there are moments when Gaskin rises to the heights of sublimity.

II

The next report came from Bob.

How can I describe Bob, if you have not met him in our previous chronicles?[1] A patron of the arts? A dilettante? The life and soul of the party? A middle-aged man of quiet elegance, with greying hair and a flickering smile? He is all these things. Perhaps his eyes are the best clue to his character. They are remarkable eyes. There is more than a hint of melancholy in them, but there are also brilliant points of light which seem to sparkle when he exercises his somewhat acid wit.

Three more things about Bob and you will have a fair picture of him.

Firstly, he is rich — at least, the majority of his friends think so, for most of his best friends are not.

Secondly, he has a highly individual vocabulary, particularly in the use of adjectives. For example, I can think of nobody but Bob who would have referred to Our Rose's dog as 'that rancid Alsatian'. And I shall always remember the occasion when a Jewish friend of mine, who had appealed for his sympathy in some Zionist cause, received the *riposte*, 'Don't turn your beady eyes on *me*, my dear.'

Lastly, there is the question of Bob's watch-chain. In case Bob might feel that this phenomenon should not be for public display, I will grant him that normally very little of it is visible. Merely a discreet and slender band of gold, from his waistcoat to his trouser pocket. It is when he takes it out of his pocket, with a resounding rattle, that the splendours are revealed — golden latchkeys, a watch concealed in a golden guinea, a golden tooth-pick, a golden champagne swizzle-stick, a golden match-box, golden mas-

[1] He appeared, with *éclat*, in *Merry Hall* and *Laughter on the Stairs*.

cots, and other golden and exotic objects which Bob, without the flicker of a smile, once described to me as 'the squalid necessities of life, my dear, which will certainly send one to the bottom of the sea, like a plummet, my dear, if one is ever shipwrecked.'

Disraeli might have written a long novel based on the rich and complex personality of Bob; I am obliged to compress that personality into a paragraph. The paragraph would not be complete without adding that his knowledge is deeper than he pretends, that his generosity is greater than he admits, and that the folk of Meadowstream have taken him to their hearts. Nobody could be less bucolic, but he fits most happily into the rural scene.

Bob's arrival, after his encounter with the Stromens, was so dramatic that I remember it all very clearly. It was on the following Sunday afternoon. I was in the garden, standing under the copper beech, where I had gone — for perhaps the tenth time that day — to pay my compliments to the miniature cyclamen. They had been transplanted to their new quarters earlier in the year, and there had been some anxiety as to how they would stand the move. They had not only stood it, but revelled in it, flourishing in the shade as they had never flourished in the sunlight. They were engaged in a game of hide and seek among the ferns, for the wind had risen, and the ferns swayed backwards and forwards, so that there were moments when they were almost hidden, and one only saw a gleam of pink among the green. Then the ferns sighed back again, and there they were, in little laughing groups of blossom. I decided that there were few more profitable occupations than watching cyclamen playing hide and seek; part of every day must definitely be set aside for it.

Suddenly there was the sound of a car coming down the

lane, an opulent purring of very large tyres on the gravel, and the silver fluting of the last word in motor horns. It was Bob, of course. None of my other friends have cars which make such rich noises.

I went out to meet him. He looked flushed and harassed. 'Beverley,' he said. 'I need a very large drink. At once.'

He sounded out of breath, as though he had been running. 'Of course, Bob. Is anything wrong?'

'It is, indeed. I think it had better be brandy. *Is* there any brandy in the house?'

'I expect so. But what has happened?'

He ignored the question and gave me a very 'beady' look. 'Not South African, I *trust?*'

'I don't imagine so.'

'We shall soon see.'

The brandy, fortunately, proved to be Martell. We took it into the music room, and when Bob had taken a big gulp, he leant back in his chair and said, in a hollow voice: 'I have met the Stromens.'

'What did you make of them?'

'I will tell you in a minute.' He took another gulp, and stared at the ceiling. As though speaking to himself he murmured: 'There are some things that come straight from The Pit.'

'I don't quite follow.'

'The Pit, my dear,' he repeated. 'Some things about certain people. They positively reek of sulphur. I have just come in contact with one of them.'

This was alarming. Had he detected the Stromens in some hideous form of necromancy?

He set down his glass. 'This afternoon,' he said, 'I drove down to see Miss Mint. I adore Miss Mint, and it was a lovely day. And I had a few rather squalid groceries to spare, which I thought she could use.' (Bob's idea of 'rather squalid groceries' is a hámper of chicken breasts in aspic, foie gras, and bottles of real turtle soup. These delicacies, from time to time, he deposits on Miss Mint's doorstep, with a faint air of guilt, as though he were disposing of an illegitimate baby.)

'Miss Mint was out and the front door was locked,' he continued, 'so I thought I would sit on the lawn and wait for her. The sun was very hot, so I took off my coat. It got hotter still, so I took off my shirt. It went on getting hotter, so I took off my vest and my pants, and there I was, my dear, practically in the nude, apart from a dainty little number by Charvet, which cost the *earth* considering that nobody ever sees it, when these fiends arrived.'

'The Stromens?'

'None other.'

'What did you do?'

'I grabbed the Charvet, my dear, and rose — with dignity, I hope — and wished them good afternoon. And then, as they didn't say anything, but merely gaped, I said that it was quite like the South of France, wasn't it. Which was a howling lie, because nothing . . . but *nothing*, has ever been less like the South of France.'

'And then?'

'Well, there were some sort of embarrassed burblings . . . and they explained who they were, and I explained who I was, and she patted her hair and giggled, and he rattled his cuffs with those *terrifying* links . . . enamel bulldogs, my dear, I swear it . . . and out came this unspeakable remark.'

'Please, Bob, don't keep me in suspense.'

He put his hand over his eyes. 'I'd made some inane excuse for being discovered with so few clothes on. I can't remember exactly what it was, but I think I suggested that everybody was very light-hearted in this part of the world, and that we were all children of nature when the sun came out. Whereupon he laughed, and gave an extra rattle to those ghastly bulldogs, and said. . . .'

Once again he paused.

'Bob, this is sheer cruelty.'

'He pointed to his wife, who is called Priscilla. And he said: "You needn't worry about me or Pris." "Pris," I ask you!'

'But that's not very terrible.'

'I haven't finished. You needn't worry about *us*, he said, because we love sunbathing too. Or words to that effect. Then it came. "In fact," he said, "if you're lucky, you'll probably find Pris lying out on the lawn in the . . ." '

'In the what?'

'No. It's impossible to repeat.'

'Bob, I can't stand this.'

He took a last gulp of brandy. Then, speaking as though his mouth were full of hot chestnuts, he gulped:

'In the full bra.'

III

There was silence.

And a strange, awful sense of indecency.

'In the *what?*'

The question was a sort of nervous twitch. I was under no illusion as to what Bob had said; it was simply that my mind, for the moment, refused to accept it.

There is nothing inherently improper about the word 'brassière' — though, as a bachelor, I always find myself confusing it with 'brasserie' and thinking of French cafés. Brassières are convenient, and in some cases essential refinements of civilization, and without them we might

89

sometimes wonder, at evening parties, whether we had not strayed back into the jungle, and whether our companions had not just emerged from clusters of bamboos, like the dusky ladies in the photographs in *Life*.

Indeed, the only reasonable objection which a moderate man could take to the brassière is that it has been elevated, by modern commerce, into a totem; it has been flourished in the face of the world as a symbol of all that is desirable and necessary to mankind. When a manufacturer of motor cars wishes to sell me his product, he does not tell me how fast it will go, nor how much petrol it uses, nor what is the cubic capacity of the engine . . . not that I should understand him if he did; he thinks it enough to find a brassière, stick something blonde inside it, and then to arrange the brassière and its occupant in an alluring position, with legs crossed, on the radiator.

Well, it is not enough for *me*. When I buy a motor car . . . or a tube of toothpaste or a packet of cigarettes . . . I am unaffected by brassières, or their occupants. I do not need them, and I wish they would get the hell out of it. The most monstrous case that I ever encountered of brassière salesmanship was in a bulb catalogue. The advertisement was for a cheap line in Dutch snowdrops. There, at the bottom of the page, was a small patch of snowdrops, looking very pale and forlorn. And over them, in brilliant colour, was this enormous brassière, with an outsize Aryan female bursting out of it, holding a snowdrop between her teeth. She should have been slapped; she should have been sent packing. I wanted snowdrops, I don't want great rollicking trollops from Amsterdam stamping all over the place, like erotic jellies. Such creatures play a very different part in one's life, if they play it at all, and a much less profitable one.

So now perhaps you will understand how that phrase — 'the full bra' — affected me.

'We really shall have to do something about them,' said Bob.

IV

Often, when I am writing a novel, I find myself envying the film director; he has at his disposal so many techniques for saving him trouble. Thus, if he wishes to indicate a lapse of time he merely has to show a calendar with its pages blowing away in the wind. And if, despite this lapse, he wishes to retain a sense of continuity, he need only repeat the final sentence in his last sequence, in a slightly different tone of voice.

Let us see what happens if, for once, we adopt this technique. We hold the camera on Bob, saying, 'We shall have to do something about them.' Then we show the leaves blowing off our calendar — nearly a hundred of them. Then we switch back to Bob . . . but no. It will not quite work. The scene makes no sense unless we mention that during this interval of time Miss Mint fell gravely ill, and it was because of her illness that things came to such a pass. Marius was away on one of his missions and I was so engaged that I did not realize what was happening. On the few occasions when I visited Miss Mint in hospital she gave no hint that anything was wrong.

It was Bob, once again, who was the indirect means of bringing things to a head, for his car, driven by the admirable and expert Alphonse, collided with the Stromens' at the bottom of the lane.

'And if Alphonse were not an absolute genius, my dear, with a nerve of *steel*, we should both be mincemeat,' he said, as he walked up the steps, rattling his chains with indignation. He turned to Alphonse. 'Va chercher Monsieur Gaskin, Alphonse, et il te donnera une fine.' Alphonse disappeared to the back door. Another rattle. 'You don't mind? He really deserves it.'

His account of the accident was vague but graphic. 'The man was driving like something *possessed*, my dear.'

'What sort of car?'

'How should I know what sort of car? All I know is that it was one of those cheap cars with its bottom where its face should have been. Which also applies to Mr. Stromen, when one comes to think of it.'

Another rattle of the chains. By now we were in the music room. Bob's eagle eye fell on a little Victorian paper-weight standing on the window-ledge. For a moment the Stromens were forgotten. Confronted by any *objet d'art*, however insignificant, Bob has no thought of anything else.

'This is charming.'

'I think so.'

He examined the base. 'I suppose you know that it is worth twenty pounds?'

'I should have said fifty.'

He looked at me out of the corner of his eyes. He allowed himself a smile. 'I always said you had a touch of the blood.'

He put down the paper-weight and threw himself into a chair. He heaved a deep sigh. 'But these Stromens. We really shall have to do something about them.'

So there we are. The film technique has worked. The leaves have been blown from the calendar, the camera is still fixed on Bob, and he has repeated the final sentence in the last sequence, all in accordance with the best Hollywood traditions.

Therefore the drama may now take a swifter turn. And

at precisely that instant, it did. The door opened and Gaskin admitted Miss Mint herself. A very pale, subdued Miss Mint, who looked as if she ought to be still in bed. From the first moment, it was obvious that something was wrong. She was twisting her fingers, and her nice, kind mouth was puckered, as though she were trying not to cry. This did not seem to be an occasion for the polite preliminaries of conversation, so I asked her at once if there was anything the matter.

'Is it about the Stromens, Miss Mint?'

'Yes, I'm afraid it is.'

'What is the trouble?'

'They . . . they do not seem to care to pay their rent.'

A fierce rattle of chains came from the sofa. 'Not *care* to pay their rent?' exploded Bob. 'Really, I find that a very curious way of putting it!' He suddenly realized that Miss Mint needed soothing rather than reproving, and his natural kindliness reasserted itself. 'How much are they in arrears?'

She fumbled in her bag, and drew out a piece of paper, which trembled in her hand. 'I think it will be four months next Tuesday.'

'Four months?' It was my turn to explode. 'But they've only *been* there four months!'

'And one week,' corrected Miss Mint. 'They did pay for the one week. In advance. I suggested that myself.' There was a sort of timid challenge in her voice, as though she wished to remind us of her business acumen.

Then she went on: 'It is not really the money which I care about so much, though it would have been very useful. What I really want them to do is to *go*. Oh! I *do* so want them to go!'

'In that case, surely all you have to do is to give them notice?'

'I *have* given them notice, but they pay no attention to it. And when I spoke to Mr. Stromen about it, he was really quite offensive. He told me to go home and read my contract.'

Bod pricked up his ears. 'What did he mean by that?'

'I'm afraid he meant . . .' She broke off, and fumbled again in her bag. 'I have the contract here. I thought that perhaps you might be kind enough to glance at it.'

'Of course.' Bob took the document and spread it out on his knees. For a few moments there was silence, except for the soft purrs of 'Four' on Miss Mint's lap. 'Four' always seems to know when there is trouble in the air, and appears at crucial moments, like a sort of feline district visitor, to offer the solace of his purr, which is perhaps the most soothing sound now echoing in this distracted world.

Then Bob looked up with a smile. 'My dears,' he said, 'we can all relax. You can turn them out tomorrow. Listen to this. Clause Six. "If the rent should be in arrears for a period of not less than two weeks, *whether it is demanded or not*, the landlord may enter and take possession." ' He threw down the contract on the sofa. 'Nothing could be simpler.'

Miss Mint merely sighed.

Bob stared at her. 'You don't seem to be exactly over-joyed.'

'I'm afraid it is not quite so simple as that.'

'You don't mean to tell me that you've signed any other document?'

'No. But you see, that contract refers to a furnished tenancy. And now, Mr. Stromen says. . . .'

Then the whole sorry story came out. Mr. Stromen was evidently better acquainted than Miss Mint with the complex laws that determine the privileges of the British landlord. One of these laws, as most readers are probably aware, makes it impossible for a landlord to evict his tenants from unfurnished premises. As long as the premises are furnished, however sparsely, the landlord is on safe ground, and can rid himself of an undesirable tenant by the simple process of giving him notice. But if they are unfurnished, no power on earth can get them out, as long as they pay their rent. Indeed, they need not even do that, for they may appeal against the rent, and take the case to court, and get dozens of people involved in an unholy mess of Bumbledom.

But how, you may ask, could this concern Miss Mint? Had she not let her cottage *furnished*?

This was precisely the question that Bob asked her.

'The cottage was furnished, wasn't it?'

'To begin with, yes.'

'How do you mean . . . "to begin with"? They haven't run off with the furniture, have they?'

'No. But the day after they moved in, they asked me if I could take away a few things to make room for a very large cocktail cabinet which they had bought. I felt I could hardly refuse. The week after, Mrs. Stromen came to me, and said that her mother had given her a bedroom suite, and would be so hurt if they did not use it. So I was obliged to turn out all my things from the bedroom, and store them in the barn.'

'Obliged!' grunted Bob.

'Yes . . . I am afraid I have been very weak. And so it has gone on, all the weeks that I have been ill. And now there is practically nothing of mine left in the cottage at all, except a few prints and a needlework rug, and when I saw Mr. Stromen, he said that the cottage was not furnished at all, and implied that it never had been furnished, and was really most discourteous and . . . and slammed the door

in my face. It looks as though they will be there for
ever. . . .'

Her voice had grown querulous; it had suddenly become
the voice of a very old, very frightened little lady. And one
tear, just one, trickled slowly down her cheek. I watched it,
with great distress, but also with that strange, abstracted
curiosity which the reasoning brain sometimes gives to
trifles in moments of crisis . . . the same curiosity which, at
a funeral, impels one to follow the flight of a feather over
the grave of somebody one has loved, even as the coffin is
being lowered. Would Miss Mint notice the tear? Would
she wipe it off? If she did not wipe it off, how far would it
get? These urgent, distracting questions were answered,
even as I watched. The tear descended in a quick silver
streak, and fell straight on to the black glistening back of
'Four'. 'Four's' action was immediate, and . . . from the
social point of view . . . impeccable, as one would have
expected from so sensitive a creature. He turned his head,
gazed for one moment at Miss Mint with his immense
green eyes, and then very gently licked his back. Never for
a moment did he stop the quiet organ music of his purr,
and as his small pink tongue made its expert strokes, he
seemed to be reminding us that grief is transient, that it
can be smoothed away in a very little while, and that all
that is needed is to trust in God and keep on purring . . . as
Oliver Cromwell might have said, if his mother had been
born a cat, which, most unfortunately, she was not.

V

'It looks as though they will be there for ever,' Miss Mint
had said, sitting in the music room with 'Four' on her lap.
As the days went by, and lengthened into weeks, it

seemed as though she might be right. The reader may find this a puzzling situation. I did myself. Here, surely, was a clear-cut case of breach of contract. The Stromens had taken Miss Mint's cottage on specific conditions; they had failed to fulfil those conditions; therefore, surely, they could be evicted? The law did not take so simple a view. Miss Mint's legal adviser was a very old gentleman, a distant relation, who seemed befuddled by the whole business. When he answered letters at all, which was seldom, they were typed in purple ink on a very old machine in which the letter P sometimes got stuck to the letter I, with bizarre results. I remember one letter which began: 'Pi am in recepipt of your letter of the seventh pinst.' This made it difficult to get a clear view of the facts. In addition, he had lost Miss Mint's inventory of the furniture, which the Stromens had signed, thereby greatly weakening her case, as it was her only definite proof that the cottage had been furnished when she let it.

It sounds absurd, it sounds utterly illogical and totally unnecessary, but that was how it was. If Miss Mint had been a less timid character, or if she had employed a more efficient adviser, things might have been different. As it was, the Stromens seemed in complete command of the situation. They made no attempt to pay the rent, they ignored the solicitor's letters, and they returned no answer to Miss Mint's diffident notes. They had not even the decency to keep themselves in the background; on the contrary, they came and went in their flashy car at all times of the day and night; they kept their radio blaring all day long, with the windows open, and they entertained quantities of their excruciatingly common friends till the small hours.

However, even Miss Mint was beginning to show faint

signs of revolt. One afternoon I was going for a walk with Bob when we met her at the corner of the lane. Miss Emily was with her, and it was she who introduced the subject of the Stromens.

'If they were on *my* property,' she snorted, 'I should turn them out with my own hands.'

For once in a way I found myself agreeing with Miss Emily. 'I should have thought you could have had the bailiffs in.'

'Not merely bailiffs, my dear,' said Bob. 'Bum bailiffs. I have no idea what bum bailiffs are, but they sound madly aggressive.'

'My solicitor says that it is too soon to take that sort of action,' sighed Miss Mint.

'Your solicitor should be . . .' I did not finish the sentence. It was no use upsetting her.

It was then that Miss Mint showed her first sign of revolt. 'I do not wish to be uncharitable,' she said gently, 'but sometimes it really does seem as if they were trying to provoke me, quite deliberately.'

'*Quite* deliberately,' echoed Miss Emily. 'Their sunbathing alone is a proof of that.'

'You don't mean to say that they have the effrontery to sunbathe?'

'Oh yes. Just at the bottom of the garden, where I cannot help seeing them.' A faint pink coloured her pretty cheeks. 'With very little on.'

'They are quite shameless,' agreed Miss Emily. 'It would be bad enough to appear like that even if one had paid one's rent, but as it is . . .' She paused, leaving us to ponder, in our separate ways, the somewhat abstruse connection between sunbathing and solvency.

A rattle of chains reminded us of the presence of Bob.

'In that case,' he suggested, 'there is only one thing to do. We must all sunbathe, too. Right in their faces.'

A frosty look from Miss Emily did not deter him. 'I am quite prepared to parade in front of them with nothing on but a *bead*, my dear. Which, though I say it myself, might bring matters to a head.'

'I hardly think. . . .'

'No, perhaps you are right.' The chain-rattling was now reaching a crescendo, which was a sure proof that Bob had been seized with an idea. He turned to Miss Mint with a charming smile. 'Why don't you leave it all to *me*, my dear? Why don't you put it all in the hands of your tiny friend?' (It should be explained that Bob, when he is about to perform some generous action — and he performs a great many — is inclined to refer to himself as 'your tiny friend'.)

'It would be very kind of you, but. . . .'

'It would be more than kind, my dear, it would be positively angelic. But that happens to be just the way your tiny friend is made. So is that settled?'

Poor Miss Mint was looking very confused. She was devoted to Bob, but she could not quite keep pace with him. She glanced from him to Miss Emily, and from Emily to me, trying to think of what she ought to say.

Bob came to her rescue. 'Of course it is settled. And now, my dears, we will resume our walk. And you will hear from me in the morning.'

He seized my arm, and we left the ladies.

'What is in your mind, Bob?' I asked, when we had turned the corner.

'Hatred, I think.' He had ceased to be the jester. 'Hatred of those vulgar beasts who are persecuting that dear old thing.'

'But what can you *do*?'

99

'If I have a free hand, quite a lot.' He smiled. 'This is one of those occasions when it is agreeable to have a little money in the bank. You ask me what I can do. I can employ the best lawyers. I can hire fleets of private detectives. If necessary, I can engage a troupe of performing seals, and set them to work, till further notice, on the Stromens's doorstep. I can make life intolerable for them. But, of course, it all depends on whether I have a free hand.'

Bob got his free hand. That night Miss Mint telephoned, in a state of the utmost distress. Her black kitten, who was named Othello, had just limped in through her door with an ugly gash on its leg. Only a few minutes before there had been an uproar at the bottom of the garden, where the Stromens were giving a party. There had been human yells and cat-calls, and screams of laughter, and there had been a brick that had landed on the lawn. Then the kitten had limped in.

'I have no proof,' she said in a trembling voice, 'but. . . .'
I did not wait for more.
'This settles it,' I said. 'Bob can go ahead?'
A long pause. And then . . . 'I should be very grateful.'
'It would be better if you were out of the way.'
Another long pause. 'Perhaps it would. I could go to my sister's.'
'And Othello?'
'Emily will take him.'

So there it was. The stage was set. On the following day, Othello went to take up temporary residence at Miss Emily's, Miss Mint departed to her sister's, and Beechnut Cottage was closed.

Meanwhile the Stromens flourished, like the monstrous cuckoos that they were. But their hours were numbered.

Bob had got to work.

VI

It was three days later when the curtain rose on the last act of this teacup tragi-comedy.

In the morning Bob telephoned, and asked me if I was disengaged during the afternoon. There was a note of subdued excitement in his voice. I told him that I had no plans. What had he in mind?

'We are going to pay a call on the Stromens.'

'On the Stromens? But Bob. . . .'

'It is all arranged. Your tiny friend has been busy.'

'But supposing they won't see us?'

'They will.'

'But supposing they aren't at home?'

'That would save a lot of trouble. And please don't argue. Your tiny friend will be with you at three o'clock.'

The morning's work was not very productive; my mind kept wandering to the approaching meeting, which promised to be unpleasant, to say the least of it. I could not imagine what Bob's plans might be. It was hardly possible that in the brief space of three days he had managed to get in motion the complicated process of evicting the Stromens by means of the bailiffs, or, indeed, by any sort of legal means. Was it possible that he intended to carry out his threat of importing a troupe of performing seals?

I was soon to know. At three o'clock precisely there was a loud hooting in the lane. I hurried to the front door. An astonishing sight met my eye. Three vehicles had drawn up in front of the house. The first was Bob's streamlined Rolls, from which he was at that moment alighting. The second was an old-fashioned Ford, in which sat two of the toughest customers I have ever seen. Both had cloth caps, both had broken noses, both had ferocious expressions, and — as far as I could see, on this first brief inspection — there was no physical difference whatever between them, apart from the fact that one was parchment white and the other was jet black.

The third vehicle was an immense wagon, in which there sat a substantial young man, grinning at nothing in particular.

'Here we are, my dear,' proclaimed Bob, walking up the steps, 'me and my tiny friends. I hope you are glad to see us.'

I drew him into the hall. 'But, Bob, where on earth did you find those people?'

'I didn't get them at Harrods, my dear, if that is what you mean.'

'What are they going to do?'

'I should think that in all probability they are going to cut our throats; but as they will cut the Stromens' first, we must put up with that.' His eye fell on a small china figure which I had just bought. He pounced on it and examined the base. 'A very nice piece of Lowestoft.'

'I thought it was Coleport.'

'No, my dear. Lowestoft. About 1810. If it weren't cracked I would make you an offer for it. And you mustn't feel nervous about my tiny friends. Alphonse found them, and he assures me that they are lambs. But positive *lambs*. Shall we go?'

I followed him to the car, glancing as I did so at the black lamb. He was picking his teeth and his lips were bared in a ferocious grin. By his side sat the white lamb. He was picking his nose and his lips were set in an equally ferocious scowl.

The next hour passed in a sort of daze. Within twenty minutes we had arrived at Oakapple Cottage. The little lane was deserted, and everything looked very peaceful. There were some moments of acute tension after Bob had rung the bell, but it jangled through an empty house. The Stromens were not at home. Moreover, they had not even locked the door. It opened as soon as Bob turned the handle. I remember feeling a slight sensation of relief. If we were all going to prison for illegal entry, the sentences might be slightly less if we had not actually broken in.

'Come along, my dears,' shouted Bob, beckoning us inside. The lambs needed no encouragement. They lumbered in after him. For a moment I hesitated. I could not have approved more passionately of what Bob was doing. For weeks, in my dreams, I had been doing this very thing — evicting the Stromens. I had done worse. In imagination I had kidnapped them, stripped them, tarred and feathered them, and thrown them, screaming with agony, into the icy waters of the Thames. So this small matter of seizing their furniture and turning them out should not really have worried one.

And yet it did. It was a question of publicity. If you are one of those people whose name is familiar to the public, whenever you do anything unorthodox, it gets into the papers. Only once have I exceeded the speed limit, but this crime was celebrated on the front page of the *Evening News*, mixed up with the arrival of Mary Pickford, which seemed to show a distorted sense of values. I did not care to speculate on what the *Evening News* might make of the present situation. Author breaks into Dream Cottage. Negro Apprehended. Mystery of French Chauffeur. The Missing Governess. It would be a field day for the *Evening News*, but it might not be so agreeable for me. This sort of episode does not increase one's prestige with the Committee of the Book of the Month.

However — in for a penny, in for a pound. It was too late to draw back. Already the lambs were squeezing through the front door with the first of the objects to be seized — a large and extremely repulsive divan covered in apricot silk. It looked as though it weighed a ton but they carried it nonchalantly, with one hand; it might have been a deck chair. At the same time, a number of cushions, in shades of mauve and sickly pink, came hurtling through one of the top windows, followed by a strange object like a doll that landed on top of the yew hedge. I went to collect it. It *was* a doll — one of those horrifying little crinoline figures that film stars used to put over their telephones. It was dreadful to think of such a contraption finding its way into Miss Mint's cottage.

And then, just as I was about to throw it into the van, I heard the shrill hoot of a car approaching at high speed. It was Mr. Stromen's, and a moment later he was turning the corner at the bottom of the lane. He always took this corner very fast, keeping one hand on the steering wheel and pressing the other on the horn. The car shot towards us and drew up with a screech of brakes in a cloud of dust. Out of it he jumped, and strode towards us. For the moment he had not noticed the presence of the lambs, who were hidden from him by the lorry. His fists were clenched and his eyes were blazing; he looked a very ugly customer.

'What the hell . . .' he shouted . . . and again, 'What the hell . . .' Whereupon words failed him. For at this precise moment Bob emerged from the front door, carrying Mrs. Stromen's squirrel coat over his arm. There was a faint smile on his face, and he looked entirely unruffled. He went straight over to Mrs. Stromen, who was standing behind her husband, with her silly mouth agape.

'I think,' he said in the politest of accents, 'that this piece of rather squalid cat must belong to you.' With a single gesture he tossed the coat over her shoulder.

She clutched it and gasped: 'Who are you? What's happening?' She plucked at her husband's sleeve. 'What are these people doing?'

'It's pretty obvious what they're trying to do,' he growled.

'In that case,' replied Bob calmly, 'we shall be saved a great deal of tedious explanation.' Out of his pocket came the gold chain, which he swung slowly backwards and forwards. In spite of the elegance of his appearance and the apparent languor of his movements, he somehow contrived to invest this glittering object with a sense of the greatest menace; it might have been a cosh or a bicycle chain.

There was a moment's silence. It was broken by the shrill voice of Mrs. Stromen. 'I don't understand. What's going on?'

'You are being evicted for non-payment of rent, my dear,' replied Bob, 'in case it had escaped your notice.'

Stromen appeared to have been momentarily stunned, but he suddenly recovered. He pushed his face up to Bob's. 'Listen to me, you,' he spluttered, 'whoever you are. If you think you can get away with this, you're making one hell of a mistake. I suppose it's that old woman who put you up to it. Well, she'll regret it, and so will you, to the end of your days. And now, mister, perhaps you'll step out of my way.'

He raised his arm in a threatening gesture. Bob remained quite still. In the gentlest of voices he said: 'I don't believe you've met my tiny friends?'

Stromen stared at him for a moment. Then he turned his head. As he did so, Mrs. Stromen clutched his arm and screamed.

Stepping slowly towards them from the shadow of the lorry were the lambs. They moved with a sort of ape-like prowl; their shoulders were hunched; their arms hung loosely at their sides; and they were both grinning. They were figures calculated to strike terror into the bravest of hearts.

Bob held up his hand. 'Just a moment, my dears,' he murmured.

The lambs halted, with evident reluctance.

Stromen made a show of bracing his shoulders. 'Rough stuff, eh?'

Mrs. Stromen clutched his arm more tightly. 'I've seen some dirty tricks in my time . . .' she began, in a trembling voice.

'Yes, my dear,' interrupted Bob, 'I'm quite sure you have. One day you must tell us all about them. In the meantime . . .' he waved his arm towards the cottage, whence the lorry-driver, who appeared to be unconscious of any drama, was staggering with a brightly polished piece of neo-Tudor furniture . . . 'in the meantime, you are preventing this young gentleman from disposing of this sluttish commode.'

She took a step forward. 'My cocktail cabinet!'

Stromen put his hand on her arm. 'Forget it.'

'But my cocktail cabinet. . . .'

'Forget it, I tell you.' There was a snarl in his voice. He turned to Bob. 'O.K. mister. You win for the moment. But you'll be hearing from us.' He swung round, with an attempt at bravado. 'You'll be hearing from us,' he repeated.

'I think not, Mr. Gross.'

Rupert Brooke once wrote an immortal little poem about the frozen second — a poem in which, as it were, he stopped the hands of the clock, and crystallized a moment of time into eternity. So it was when Bob murmured 'Mr. Gross'. We all remained quite still, staring, while the word 'Gross' echoed and re-echoed through our minds.

At last Bob spoke again, very quietly and deliberately, as

though he were explaining something to a wilful child. 'I don't think we shall be hearing from you, Mr. Gross. Either under your real name, or under any other. You see, Mr. Gross, I have been making inquiries about you. And I have found that you have done this sort of thing before, Mr. Gross. You have made quite a habit of it, Mr. Gross. It is a bad habit, Mr. Gross, and it is by no means your only one. And that is why I take leave to inform you that if you ever show your scabrous dial in this part of the world again, you will find yourself dealing, not with me, but with the police. For to put it frankly, Mr. Gross, I find you something of a muckworm, Mr. Gross.' He beckoned to the lambs. 'My dears!'

The lambs shuffled rapidly forward.

'Don't you dare touch him!' gasped Mrs. Stromen.

'Cut it out!' snarled Stromen. (I can only think of him by his bogus name.)

The lambs shuffled closer.

Bob shook his head. 'No, my dears. Not for the moment. I merely want you to take a good look at this person, so that you may be quite certain to recognize him again.'

The lambs took a good look. It was a hungry, almost wistful look, as of two bloodhounds who were being deprived of their prey.

Stromen could bear it no longer. He grabbed his wife's arm and stepped back, still facing the lambs. With a last attempt at bravado he shook his fist at Bob. 'You'll be hearing from us, mister,' he muttered in a thick voice. Then he turned and strode to the car. The doors slammed, the engine started, and a moment later there was nothing to remind us of the Stromens but a cloud of dust.

Bob returned his chain to his pocket. 'And that, my dears,' he said, 'is that.'

VII

We never heard from the Stromens. Bob had taken a considerable risk, for there had been no time to confirm the information which he had obtained, at great expense, from his private detective agency. However, it proved to be correct. Stromen was a crook, who had been running far too close to the wind to attempt to sail back into the quiet harbour of Meadowstream. Moreover, even if he had chosen to go to law, he would have had no case. Bob made no claim on his furniture, nor any demands for the arrears of rent.

'After all,' he said, 'what we wanted was to get rid of them, and that we have done. There is no point in being vindictive, even when one is dealing with cads, toughs, cut-throats and slubberdegullions.'

'With what, Bob?'

'Slubberdegullions, my dear. It sounds like the things they put in one's bouillebaisse, but it really means the Stromens. You should use it in one of your dainty books, and impress people with your erudition.'

Well, I have used it in one of my dainty books, and I hope you are impressed.

There is a footnote to our story — a very happy one, too.

When the cottage was cleared of the last remnants of the Stromens, Bob arranged for Miss Mint's belongings to be carried back from the barn, where they had been stored, and returned to their original positions. He also employed Alphonse and the lambs for several days, cleaning and dusting and painting and digging and clipping, so that by the end of the week Oakapple Cottage, and its tiny garden, presented such a spotless appearance that I felt it should be renamed Apple Pie Cottage.

However, this was not enough for Bob. When we went in for a final inspection he paused on the threshold. 'This doorknocker,' he observed, 'might be described as insubstantial.' (It was, in fact, a flimsy piece of rusty iron.) 'There should be something elegant. A dolphin, I think, if one can find the right sort of dolphin. I must see to it.' He stepped inside. 'And coco-nut matting, my dear, may be very nice if you intend to fill the house with a horde of Pomeranians, but it sets my teeth on edge. We could do better than that. And really, you know, my dear, there is not much to be said for that stair-carpet, and now I come to think of it, I was not very impressed by the towels in the bath-room . . . they would be all very well for a midget, but they would not be at all satisfactory for the lambs.'

'Are the lambs thinking of taking a bath?'

'I doubt if they have ever thought of taking a bath, but the idea might enter their heads, and then where should we be?'

And so it was, all over the cottage. By the time the sun was setting Bob had prepared a list covering six pages of his small notebook — (which, needless to say, was thickly encased in gold). A couple of days later he made his last trip with the lambs, and for several hours there was a great deal of hammering and shifting and turning out. When I went over in the evening, and stepped into the little hall, I felt as though somebody had waved a magic wand. A soft Bokhara rug was stretched in front of the fire-place. A pale grey self-fitted carpet had been laid on the stairs. Instead of the rickety old bamboo table by the wall there was a delicate Victorian sideboard of papier mâché. Above it there hung a pair of eighteenth-century flower pictures.

It was the same everywhere. There were new linen sheets, carefully laid out on the beds, and towels in the bathroom of such opulence that even the lambs could have had no complaints.

'It is all a lot of tat, my dear,' said Bob, standing on the Bokhara rug, which must have been worth at least fifty pounds, 'and not me at all. As you have so kindly pointed out in the past, my taste is rococo, and I am sure you are surprised that I have not gilded the beams and put luminous paint on the loo, my dear. But I tried to think what the old darling would like, and I hope I have succeeded. The only thing I could not find was the dolphin.'

But we found even that, on the very day that Miss Mint returned — a most charming and amiable creature in bronze, that had once hung over the door of an old Venetian pharmacy. We were actually hanging it up when the village taxi trundled round the corner of the lane, bringing her home. And perhaps our tale might end with this happy symbol — the dolphin hanging on the door, the door slowly opening, and a bewildered little lady standing on the threshold, and looking round her, with wide, staring eyes, and slowly understanding, and then . . . wondering whether to laugh or to cry.

CHAPTER VI

THE GOOD EARTH

I T must not be thought that Meadowstream, during
the whole of this summer, was solely concerned with
the affairs of Miss Mint; there were many other dramas
engaging, or about to engage, our attention; indeed, whenever I was obliged to visit London I had a feeling of flatness
as I stepped out at Waterloo Station; the streets of the great
city, by comparison with the lanes of Meadowstream, were
curiously devoid of human interest.

There was, for example, the growing tension between
Miss Emily and Our Rose. This was due to Rose's claims as
a spirit healer, which were becoming increasingly extravagant. The situation was explosive, and whenever the two
ladies met at our various houses, the one topic of conversation
we endeavoured to avoid was blight — or, indeed, any form
of disease which might be afflicting our gardens. Blights,
mildews, pests and even — so one gathered — such plagues

as wireworms were all quite unnecessary according to Rose, and were only a proof that the owner of the garden was not in tune with the harmonic vibrations of the universe. The effect of such theories on a severely practical woman like Miss Emily may well be imagined.

However, as we all know, when a conversational topic is taboo, it has a perverse habit of intruding itself. In spite of all our efforts, it seemed as though our minds were obsessed by one subject and only one — blight. Even if we talked of the Coronation, blight crept in. It was quite uncanny; I should not have been surprised to find myself — under some sort of hypnotic compulsion — expressing the hope that there would be no blight on St. Edward's Crown.

This passing reference to St. Edward's Crown gives me an excuse for a little aside concerning Mrs. Oldfield. That dear old lady was passionately interested in every detail of the preparations for the Coronation; she could not have been more absorbed if she had been going to be crowned herself. One day I met Oldfield in the lane and asked him how she was. He shook his head.

'Not too well, sir,' he said. ' 'Tis that stiff neck of hers.'

'Dear me! Has she been sitting in a draught?'

'No, sir. 'Tis like this. She reads in t'paper that St. Edward's Crown — I reckon that's what they call it — weighs fourteen pounds, or some such. So she gets to worrying about Her Majesty, sitting there in t'Abbey for all that time with all that weight on her head. So she goes to t'bookshelf and gets down a whole lot of books and weighs 'em, up to fourteen pounds, and down she sits with all them books on her head for four solid hours, and nothing'll budge her, not even to get my dinner. "If Her Majesty can do it," she says, "I can do it." And do it she does. But it give her a stiff neck, all the same.'

However, we were talking about blight, and how it seemed to dominate all our conversation. And that leads to yet another aside. (We might as well reconcile ourselves to the fact that this book seems to be composed of nothing but asides.) This one concerns Marius. We were all having tea with a mutual friend, and by a most unfortunate accident the tea-table had been set on the lawn, just in front of a large bed of lavender.

Now lavender, as we all know, is greatly afflicted by that inelegant complaint, cuckoospit. It cannot be described as a major plague, but it is a distasteful one, like a child with a snuffly nose. If you wipe away the spittle you will find two little beetles, spitting away like mad. They look very pale and unhealthy, which is hardly surprising in view of their habits. They run down the stem when you disturb them, and are difficult to catch.

This hedge, behind the table where we were having tea, was covered with cuckoospit, and as soon as Rose observed it, a gleam came into her eye. Here was a golden opportunity for her to vent her theories. By chance, Marius noted the gleam, and interpreted it correctly. Before Rose could say her piece he had set the talk on a course which neither she, nor any of the rest of us, could have anticipated.

'I see,' he observed to our hostess, 'that your beautiful lavender hedge is covered with cuckoospit.'

There was an embarrassed pause, and several reproachful glances at Marius. Surely he was aware of the conversational ban on blight? However, before we could change the subject, Rose had already seized her opportunity.

'So unnecessary,' she exclaimed. 'So totally unnecessary.' She leant forward and took a deep breath. She was about to mount her hobby-horse.

Marius was too quick for her. 'I quite agree with you,' he said gravely. 'It is totally unnecessary.'

Rose raised her eyebrows. She was not used to agreement; she flourished best on opposition; and it was evident that she was none too pleased with Marius's interjection.

'Ah — but you are thinking of spraying them with poisons!' she retorted. 'That is how *you* deal with these things. Whereas I. . . .'

'I am thinking of nothing of the sort,' interrupted Marius, gently but firmly. 'I am thinking of boredom.'

'Of what?'

'Of boredom, my dear madame. You can be bored to death, I can be bored to death, blight can be bored to death. Particularly cuckoospit.'

Rose bared her teeth in a very unconvincing smile. 'So amusing,' she hissed.

'But I mean it quite literally. I have almost no knowledge of entymology; I would even hesitate to express an opinion as to whether the Frog-Hopper — which is, of course, the common name for the insect which produces the cuckoospit — should be classified under the diptera or the coleoptera.'

I could see Rose wincing under the impact of these formidable words.

'Nevertheless,' continued Marius, 'I can hardly fail to be aware that the frothy substance emitted by this insect — with the object, needless to say, of protecting its larvae — is approximately six times the size of the insect itself. In short, it is obliged to spit the equivalent of six bubble baths before it can devote itself to any other occupation.'

Rose's smile remained fixed.

Marius raised his finger. 'Now here is the point. Insects are very like human beings; the studies of entymology and anthropology constantly overlap. Imagine, madame, your

Midday

own feelings if, at the beginning of each day, you were obliged to spit six bubble-baths in order to conceal your offspring.'

If Marius had not been Marius, who was a law unto himself, the ladies of Meadowstream might have found this fantasy in doubtful taste. As it was, they were fascinated.

His finger was still raised. 'Imagine, moreover, that I were then to come along, three times a day, with a hose of water, and wash away the products of your labour. You would be obliged to spit no less than eighteen bubble-baths in the course of a single day. What would be the result, madame?'

He did not wait for any reply. 'You would be bored, madame, and you would decide to leave the district,' he concluded, on a note of triumph. 'Which is precisely what has happened in the case of my own blight. I have hosed them with plain water, three times a day. They have become bored, and they have left the district.'

He turned to our hostess with a charming smile. 'And I am sure, my dear lady, that my conversation will have a similar effect on us all unless we change the subject.'

It was a skilful ruse on Marius's part; it made it quite impossible for Rose to ride her hobby-horse — at least, on that occasion.

Apart from that, his recipe works. You can hose cuckoo-spit with plain water, and they do get bored and leave the district. I know, because I have done it.

With such asides our lives were entertained, during the summer, and though they may not have been so tense as the affair of Miss Mint, they had some of the elements of drama.

However, in my own life and on my own estate, another

drama was developing, of such magnitude that all else was forgotten. This was no 'aside', no passing fancy; it was something of the greatest importance, and it still is. How important, the reader may agree, when he is informed that it involved the moving of a mountain.

In order to explain how I came to move this mountain, and why it was so essential that it should be moved, I must ask him to bear with me while I indulge in a few reflections on the basis of all gardening, and indeed of all life . . . the soil, the good earth itself.

II

It seems almost incredible, after all these years of gardening, that I had not learned the most elemental lesson of all, the absolute A.B.C. of the job. I had not learned the lesson of the soil.

I was like a pianist who could play the majority of the Chopin etudes without ever having learned how to play an arpeggio. (That, of course, would be impossible, but it roughly expresses what I mean.) I could have passed a gardening examination with reasonable honours, both in theory and in practice; my botanical vocabulary — always a test — was respectable; and if there were any tricky jobs to be done, I could usually do them.

But till now there had always been this quite inexplicable blind spot. I had ignored the soil . . . the quality of the soil, its essential nature. By which I do not mean that I had not appreciated the importance of digging and double-digging, of manuring and mulching. I mean that I had not appreciated the vital difference between a soil that is acid and a soil that is alkaline.

If you are not a gardener it is more than probable that

the above paragraph will cause you to skip, and turn over the pages in a frenzy, until you reach an oasis of dialogue. Very well, we will have some.

Reader	What is an acid soil?
B. N.	A soil that contains no chalk.
Reader	Are you sure?
B. N.	Quite sure.
Reader	It sounds to me as if it ought to be the other way about. I should have thought an acid soil would have been stiff with chalk.
B. N.	So would I. But it isn't. Acid means no chalk.

Pause, while reader wonders whether to take a bet on it, and then thinks better of it — very wisely.

Reader	Well, what difference does it make whether there's chalk in it or not?
B. N.	It makes a world of difference. It makes a universe of difference. Chalk, to the gardener, is poison. It is damnation and destruction. He should fly from it as he would fly from the plague. The very sight of the white cliffs of Dover should make him feel physically sick.
Reader	Here, steady on! The white cliffs of Dover have a very special meaning for most Englishmen.
B. N.	I can't help that. They should be blown up. At once. So should Salisbury Plain. So should anywhere with chalk in it.
Reader	(at length) *Why* is chalk so bad?
B. N.	Because it is death to at least half the loveliest things that grow from the earth. It slaughters the glorious company of rhododendrons, and it slays the brilliant hosts of azaleas. Nearly all the heathers die in it, and many of the gentians.

The elegant camellias dread it as fearfully as the humble blue poppies. The list of beautiful shrubs that wither and fall at the very touch of it would fill a book. . . .

Reader   So I gather that there is no chalk in your garden?

B. N.   On the contrary, it is full of it.

Reader   Then why on earth did you make a garden on it?

B. N.   Because I was demented. I told you, I had a blind spot.

And that was why I moved the mountain.

III

But now I must say a word in self-defence. It was not entirely my fault.

When I bought Merry Hall, nearly ten years ago, I fell in love with a house that had been nearly ruined and a garden that had relapsed into a wilderness. I was so eager to restore the house and to reclaim the garden that I did not look far into the future. It never occurred to me to analyse the soil. Why should it? The district had not a particularly chalky 'feel'; there were plenty of pines and silver birches in the fields around; in a neighbouring coppice there were wild rhododendrons; on a little hill that I could see from my bedroom window there were a few patches of purple heather. You do not find these delights where there is much chalk.

But I had reckoned without the late Mr. Stebbing.

Mr. Stebbing — for the information of those who have not followed the previous chronicles[1] — was a former owner of Merry Hall who had done his utmost to ruin it. He was a bearded monster with an oppressed wife, and I

[1] *Merry Hall* and *Laughter on the Stairs*.

can best sum him up by quoting two of his favourite occupations. Firstly, he used to play Bach on an old pianola after breakfast, not because he liked Bach, but because the action of pedalling stimulated his intestines. Secondly, he used to encourage his extremely repulsive dogs to chase cats. Each of these predilections suggests that somebody was very careless not to have strangled Mr. Stebbing at birth.

Because of Mr. Stebbing, my task at Merry Hall in the first two years was simple. I had only to ask myself what Mr. Stebbing had done, and then, to undo it. Had Mr. Stebbing erected a sinister parody of a public convenience on the south wall? Yes, he had. Very well, knock it down. Had he put in a stained glass window on the staircase, featuring a rose-pink mermaid with a triangular, beige behind? Indeed, that was just what he had done. Away with it. Had he dug a noisome pond just outside the music room, and piled all the earth from it into an obscene Charlotte Russe on the middle of the lawn? The dainty creature had done precisely that. Send for the bulldozers.

I sent for the bulldozers. I had the whole garden turned into a ploughed field. The sheet must be wiped clean; I had to start with a blank canvas. Only thus could the ghost of this horrible man be finally exorcized.

But Mr. Stebbing was stronger than I thought.

He was still lurking in the soil.

Do you know what he had done? Can you guess it?

He had filled the garden with chalk!

This fiend — his beard seems to grow blacker and more sulphurous as I write — had imported cartload upon cartload of chalk into the garden, years before my arrival, in order to cover the lawns with horrible little paths, leading to nowhere. (Chalk, being essentially poisonous, keeps down weeds.) I shall never forget the dismay with which

I returned, after a week of absence, to see the flecks of dirty white all over the ploughed earth. The ploughs had done their work all too well. Whereas the chalk, in Mr. Stebbing's time, had been restricted to a maze of paths, which could at least have been isolated, it was now scattered all over the estate. To attempt to eradicate it would have been a labour of Hercules. And yet this was the labour I was shortly to attempt. For after the disaster of the plough I went up to Wales, to stay at Bodnant. And there I met a certain flower, and fell in love, and was lost, and the whole of life was changed.

IV

Bodnant, the home of the late Lord Aberconway, is perhaps among the three most beautiful gardens in the world. It lies on a Welsh hill, and falls gently to the distant river Conway, terrace by terrace, walk by winding walk. It has every natural advantage of which a gardener could dream; but history has been as kind to it as nature. For nearly a century it had only two owners, who were each wise, cultured and rich. For fifty years Lord Aberconway's mother filled the garden with treasures, and he carried on where she left off, for another fifty years. As if this were not enough, for the last years of his life he was President of the Royal Horticultural Society, which meant that gardeners from all over the world came to him with their most precious discoveries, and placed them in his care. Finally, through the institution of the National Trust, to which so many of the great houses of Britain owe their continued existence, he was enabled to employ labour on a scale that would otherwise have been impossible even for the richest man.

It is difficult to compete with such advantages, when one starts with a ploughed field, when one's labour force consists of a solitary octogenarian, and when . . . yes, here it is again . . . one is infested with chalk. Needless to say, in the whole glorious prospect of Bodnant there is not a grain of chalk. Not a spoonful of the evil stuff.

It was a hot August afternoon, with thunder in the air, when I arrived at Bodnant, and I am afraid that my behaviour was not in accordance with the traditions of polite society. For when I had rung the bell, I happened to glance over my shoulder, and what I saw compelled me to dart down the steps and across the drive, where I concealed myself in a rhododendron bush. A moment later the door opened, and a bemused butler stared at my empty car. Then he shrugged his shoulders and closed the door again. Which left me free to explore.

The reason for this eccentric behaviour was that when I had glanced over my shoulder, I had seen my first Eucryphia, and the impact was so shattering that it would have been quite impossible to go in and meet the family, and make polite conversation, until one had got one's breath. One would have made no sense. One would have stared out of the window, muttering Eucryphia, Eucryphia. If anybody had asked one if one wanted to wash one's hands, one would have replied that one was madly anxious to wash one's Eucryphia, which might have been misconstrued.

Do you know the Eucryphia? Unless you live on peat the answer may be 'No'. Which is a pity for all concerned, as I shall now be obliged to describe it. And as you may have gathered, the very thought of the Eucryphia makes my blood-pressure rise, and fills my brain with a buzz of superlatives. Nevertheless I shall try, even if it ends in tears.

The Eucryphia is summer snow. It is spring blossom in

the heavy, sultry months, when the year is middle-aged. At a time when all the trees in the valley are staid and set, and when some of their leaves are already flecked with the sad stains of autumn, the Eucryphia arrives . . . young and gay and white . . . like a girl who has come late to a party, and the revels begin all over again. That was how I came to feel, standing on the terrace at Bodnant, on a summer evening, looking down into the valley. The summer trees were dark and stately, like dowagers at a reception. They were invested with an immense dignity, they knew their position, and their conversation was carried on in sighs and whispers, beech to beech, cedar to cedar, pine to pine. And then, in danced the Eucryphias, with a flutter of gauze, a wisp of silver lace, up hill and down dale. . . .

I told you that it would end in tears.

What is the actual flower like? That is easy to answer. It is exactly like a white St. John's Wort; the only difference is that it is a St. John's Wort flowered in heaven, with the divine radiance still glowing in its petals. Oddly enough, in spite of this resemblance, it has nothing to do with the St. John's Wort family. If you look it up in Mr. Bean[1] — and it is always wise to look things up in Mr. Bean — you will find these authoritative and strangely evocative words: *'The genus is of peculiar botanical interest in having no known close allies, and its true place in the vegetable kingdom is doubtful. It is sometimes placed in the Rose family.'*

I wonder if I am alone in hearing, in those words, a whole chorus of musical echoes and shadowy suggestions of beauty? They could not be more practical and down-to-earth; and yet, if a poet had ever encountered them, a poet

[1] *Trees and Hardy Shrubs in the British Isles.* By W. J. Bean, Late Curator, Royal Botanic Gardens, Kew. Three volumes. John Murray.

like Coleridge — yes, it would have to be Coleridge — he might have been transported on a journey to fairyland. The white lonely flower, blooming in solitude in the dark woods, and in the distance the glimmer of a rose. . . .

V

For three days I walked about Bodnant in a haze, sometimes alone, usually with Lord Aberconway. He was an ideal cicerone, wearing his erudition as lightly as a scarf. I cannot have made much sense; I was torn by too many conflicting emotions. There was a most unchristian covetousness at the thought of this mountain of dark, sweet, fragrant earth, with its terraces, its fountains, and its scented glades; there was a murderous hatred of the ghost of Mr. Stebbing and his legacy of chalk; there was sheer despair at the thought of all the time I had wasted. Above all there was the bewilderment engendered by vista upon vista of sheer beauty. Just as one was recovering from a sweep of rose-pink heathers one would be knocked silly by a crowd of auratums or dizzied by the reflection, in a pool, of bank upon bank of blue and purple hydrangeas. (Obsessional note. Hydrangeas, needless to say, require an acid soil. With chalk you can do nothing with them, even if you deluge them with patent mixtures, and pour cartloads of rusty nails round them. They remain a firm and to me, extremely vulgar pink, like cheap marshmallows.)

'Could I grow that?' I would ask, time and again, as we encountered some new splendour.

'I'm afraid not,' Lord Aberconway would reply. 'It does not tolerate lime.'

'Or that?'

'No. It is also a lime-hater.'

'Or that?'

He shook his head. 'You should concentrate on things which *will* tolerate lime.'

'I'm sure I should.'

He smiled. 'And I'm equally sure you won't. You're like all of us; you love a good fight.'

'If I imported the right soil . . . could I grow a Eucryphia? Just one?'

'You'd need a lot of it. You'd also need to isolate it from the rest of the soil, so that the limy water wouldn't percolate to the roots. That would mean a protected pit, with adequate drainage, or some form of elevation. It would all be extremely expensive.'

But in theory, at least, it would be possible?'

'In theory, of course. And in gardening, if you want a thing badly enough, you often end by growing it. I sometimes think it's partly a question of faith — the sort of faith that, according to Christabel, will move mountains.'

He had said it. The idea was born. And I like to think that as he spoke, there was a faint tremor, far away in the south, in the hills that stretched beyond Merry Hall.

I left Bodnant with a car laden with treasures. There was a fine Viburnum Fragrans, a new variety of which there were only a dozen in the world. And pots of Lapagerias, and roots of irises and boxes of a delicious little hardy cyclamen, which was much paler than the common variety. They have all flourished in my garden, for they all tolerate lime.

But there was something else in the car, something which nobody gave me. I stole it. It was a clump of the magical soil of Bodnant. I stuffed my sponge-bag with it, and hid it in the boot. I looked on it as a token, the beginning of a new adventure. And that was what it proved to be.

CHAPTER VII

AN END AND A BEGINNING

W HEN I came back from Bodnant, I emptied the
soil from the sponge-bag, and placed it in a box,
and took it out into the garden, and set it under
the copper beech, and put a little glass over the top.

Then I stepped back and regarded it, feeling rather like
those people in pantomimes who stride on to the stage with
some magic token which has only to be rubbed between
their fingers in order to effect a transformation scene.
You know the sort of thing . . . Abracadabra — and lo, the
empty garret becomes, in a flash, a fairy palace with fountains entirely surrounded by blondes, standing on their
heads, pretending to be lupins, but looking, oddly enough,
very much like blondes standing on their heads.

I really did see visions, hovering round that little box. I
saw great clusters of purple, from rhododendrons yet un-
planted, and sheets of flame from ghostly azaleas and even

. . . glimmering on the far horizons of my imagination . . . the distant snows of the Eucryphias. If you think that those visions were unwarranted, let me assure you, with some authority, that they were not. In due course those visions were fulfilled. From that little box — or rather, from the vast quantities of soil which I caused to be assembled round the nucleus of that little box — there did spring great clusters of purple and sheets of flame. If anybody is inclined to deny it, I have photographs to prove it. Admittedly, they were taken in a faint mist, and the persons who were induced to pose in front of them, to give 'perspective', were all chosen because of their approximation to midgets. None the less, they are extremely effective photographs, calculated to silence the criticism of all but the most carping.

So there I stood, seeing my visions.

But I saw something else, too. I saw 'One', my Siamese cat.

He came towards me slowly, but deliberately, from the shadows of the copper beech, where he had been sleeping. It was, of course, his duty to do so. Every parcel that had ever arrived at Merry Hall, every crate of bulbs, every load of manure . . . indeed, every importation of any sort whatever . . . had to be inspected by 'One'. It had to be sniffed, and prowled around, and dabbed with a tentative paw, and . . . especially if one was in a hurry . . . it had to be sat upon. Or, if he were being more than usually provoking, laid upon, upside down, with his paws crossed over his chest.

So naturally 'One' had to come out from the shadows of the copper beech to inspect the magic box of earth.

'No,' I said to 'One', 'it is not that sort of box.'

For he had scraped the top of it with his paw.

He looked up at me with his blue eyes . . . still dazzling, though they were growing old. He gave a faint wail.

'And it's sheer affectation, "One", my dear,' I said, 'to

pretend that you want a box in the middle of the garden. The whole world is your box.'

Another wail.

'It is like sailing out into the middle of the lake at Evian,' I persisted, 'and demanding that somebody should supply you with water from a bottle.'

'One' . . . who always responded to civilized arguments . . . gave a final wail. But it was on a downward scale, indicating assent.

We walked back to the house together. The little box stayed there under the copper beech. Dreams were clustering around it, in the falling light. And in the weeks to come, I was glad of those dreams. For they often helped me to forget that 'One' . . . was dying.

II

If you are among those who think that paper and ink should not be wasted on so slight a matter, you will turn the page. I am obliged, however, to write about it, if only to ease my own conscience. You see, in the end he had to be 'put away', and it was I who had to give the final decision. And I still feel like a murderer. I believe I was right . . . and yet . . . and yet! There are times when one hopes, most earnestly, that there is no such place as the conventional heaven, or — if there is — that one will not have the *entrée* to it. I do not know how I should be able to look 'One' in the face, if he were sitting anywhere near the pearly gates on my arrival. He almost certainly *would* be sitting near them. He was a great one for sitting near gates, watching people come in and out. How would he look at me, with those sapphire eyes? Would he understand? Or would he say to himself, 'Here is that man who took me from my garden, and put me in a basket, and sent me away on my last journey'? Having said that, would he slowly turn, and walk away up the golden steps, and vanish for ever into that beige and blue department of heaven which, one imagines, is reserved for Siamese cats?

It hardly bears thinking of. Yet most owners of pets who have been forced to take this decision cannot help thinking of it. I expect that they try to comfort themselves with the thought that if only their pets could understand, they would realize that their masters had acted from love, that they had tried to do what was kindest.

Most assuredly this was so in the case of 'One'. We need not go into details. It is enough that he was in almost constant pain, and that there was no hope of his ever being better. I cannot remember when we decided that the time had come to put an end to his sufferings. I do not think that we ever said it, in so many words. It was more like a shadow, falling across the lawn. It was there; we could not escape it.

It was almost worse for Gaskin than for me. We both loved 'One', but it was Gaskin who had fed him, brushed him, dosed him, and nursed him through his illnesses. I tried to comfort Gaskin.

'At least we can remember this,' I said. 'If it hadn't been for us, and in particular for you, "One" would have been dead seven years ago.'

'I wonder,' said Gaskin.

'The vet. told us that,' I persisted. 'Time and again he said it. If we hadn't sat up with him at nights, and if you hadn't been so good with all those injections, which I could never have given him, he couldn't have lived.'

Gaskin shook his head. 'No, it was "One" who saved himself. He didn't want to die.'

I wished that Gaskin had not said that. It was poignantly true. Never shall I forget that crisis, seven years ago. 'One' had acute pneumonia. His heart had almost stopped. Everything that could be done had been done — apparently to no avail. He lay there in his basket, a thin, feverish shadow, so weak that when he tried to open his eyes all you could see was a thin slit of blue. When you put your face down to comfort him, he tried to purr, but he could only manage a sad little gasp.

I carried his basket into the music room, set it near the fire, and gave him a last stroke. Then I went out. I did not sleep very well that night. In the morning I got up long before Gaskin, just as the first sunlight was slanting across the deserted lawn. I went down to the music room and stood outside it. I did not want to open the door.

Then the miracle happened. From the other side of the door there had come a tiny mew. I could not believe it. But there it was again, faint but unmistakable, the strange unearthly music of the Siamese cat. I pushed open the door. There, trying to sit up in his basket, swaying unsteadily, blinking in the sunlight, was 'One'. He had fought his way out of the valley of the shadow.

But that was seven years ago. Seven years in the life of a cat is fifty years in the life of a man. It could not be like that again.

The agonizing problem remained — when? The pain was getting worse, but perhaps . . . if it were a fine September, might he not have a few last weeks of sunshine? We asked ourselves this sort of question with each new day. I had a terrible feeling that he *knew* what was in our minds. One occasion in particular lingers in my memory; there was nothing special to mark it; it is just a fragment of time that has isolated itself. I had strolled out to the water-garden, and was sitting on the wide stone steps, basking in the sunlight. After a few minutes I saw 'One' walking across the lawn to join me. He walked more slowly, nowadays, with a slight limp, but his tail was still erect. As he drew near he began to speak, according to his invariable custom. 'One' never approached me in silence. He always talked. Usually I did not pay much attention; but now I felt that he was trying to tell me something. He came nearer and nearer, still speaking, holding me with his blue eyes. He seemed to be saying that he did not want to die. Then he lay down on the stone, as he always used to do, with his front paws dangling loosely, to show that he wished to be dragged slowly on his back across the stone. But even as I bent forward to move him, he put out a paw to stop me. His back was too painful to be touched. So I just held on to his paw, and he closed his eyes, and lay there and went to sleep.

That was one of his last good days.

The end came two weeks later, after a final consultation with the vet. I was thankful that I had to be in London at the time. It was bad enough coming home, to a house that seemed so empty. 'One' had always greeted me; he would be sitting at the window, and would speak to me through the glass when I walked across to tap it; or he would come racing across the lawn, and jump on to my shoulders with a single (and rather alarming) leap; or in later days he would rise from a chair in the hall, and stretch himself . . . always speaking, in his strange, bitter-sweet voice. And now that voice was silent.

I pushed open the door of the kitchen.

'It's all over, Gaskin?'

He merely nodded. He did not feel inclined to speak. Nor did I. But I forced myself to say something about it being only a matter of a few seconds . . . and how we must remember that he didn't know what was happening.

Gaskin did not seem to hear me.

He took a deep breath. Then he said something which I shall never forget. 'The worst moment was when I had to give him his last meal.'

We looked at each other. That was when we felt like murderers.

'And now I'd rather not say any more,' said Gaskin.

III

I had not said goodbye to 'One'. It would have been quite unbearable; he would have known what I was about.

But now I wanted to say goodbye, and I knew where I must say it — in the orchard. That was where I should find the memory of him most vivdly. So I left the empty house, and walked slowly across the lawn, up to the wild grass and the old apple trees.

As I walked, I remembered how many times, in these last ten years, 'One' had been by my side. He would stay with me on the lawn, and past the rose garden, but as soon as the orchard was reached he would dash ahead, and race up the gnarled trunk of an old apple or plum, and stay there, tense with expectation, his elegant brown-gloved arms stretched round the trunk, waiting for me to come and play. There was no escape from the pleading — indeed, the compulsion — of those blue eyes. I might be tired, I might be abstracted, but I had to play. And play, too, according to a rigid code of rules. First, I had to pick a supple switch of elm or elder from the hedge, and strip it, except for a few tantalizing leaves at the end. Then I had to approach slowly through the long grass, with this plaything behind my back, and pause in front of 'One', and look up at him, while he wailed in pretended fury at the delay. And then — drama! I whip out the twig and poise it, fluttering on a branch just beyond his reach. He springs — misses it — I flutter it to another branch — he prowls, slowly, slowly — misses it again. And so on, and so on, until at last we decide — (and it really is a joint decision) — that the time for the climax has come. Whereupon, with a final swoop, he seizes the end of the twig, and climbs down the tree, while I hold on to the other end, and he drags me off to any destination he may choose, while I murmur 'One, you are a very clever cat, the cleverest cat in the whole of Surrey.' A compliment which he acknowledges with a fearsome growl.

And I think to myself, as I allow myself to be towed along, in this strange procession, dodging under the branches of trees and sweeping aside the thorny briars into which he sometimes conducts me, that it is only right and proper that a man, for a change, should be on the receiving end of a leash, that he should take direction from an animal, even if the animal is a Siamese cat — or perhaps especially if the animal is a Siamese cat. For men, when they are in command of affairs, are liable to lead us to the edge of the abyss. Whereas cats, at the worst, will only land us into a tangle of sweet briar.

The orchard was sunlit and tranquil, and the apples were already so heavy that the boughs would soon need propping up to save them from splitting. I bent down to pick up an old stake that had fallen . . . and then, suddenly, I stopped and stared. Opposite me, at the base of the trunk, was a big, bare patch where the bark had been stripped off. Some of it had been stripped so recently that there were still fragments of bark lying in the long grass.

It was 'One's' favourite scratching place — the tree that

he had chosen, even as a kitten, for sharpening his claws —
an old Cox's Orange Pippin, whose fruit was still as sweet
as it had been when it was first planted, long before I was
born.

Some instinct had guided me to it. It was there that I
whispered my goodbye to 'One', on that silent, sunlit
afternoon. I hope that he heard me.

IV

We will end on a happier note.

Back at the house, I said to Gaskin, 'We've got to snap
out of this. Otherwise it'll be bad for Four and Five. They'll
realize something is wrong.'

'They do already,' said Gaskin. He took out his handkerchief and blew his nose violently. 'Four wouldn't touch
his fish this morning. And Five only pecked at his.'

I felt that this was one of the moments when one had to
be cruel to be kind.

'That won't do them any harm,' I said. 'They're both far
too fat as it is.'

Even as I spoke, I realized that this was a most brutal
remark to make, in the circumstances. But it had to be
made. Otherwise we should spend the rest of our lives
drooping round the house, draped in crêpe.

'We must find a Six,' I said.

Gaskin shook his head. 'I couldn't face a Six,' he replied.
'Not yet, at any rate.'

'But this is just the time when we ought to be thinking
of a Six. It's like having a crash in an aeroplane. As soon
as you've had a crash, you ought to get into another
aeroplane at the earliest possible opportunity, otherwise
you lose your nerve.'

'I just couldn't think of a Six,' he repeated doggedly.

'It wouldn't be another Siamese. I couldn't think of that, either. Not for years. Just an ordinary kitten. Not a black one, because that would be unfair to Four. Not a tabby, because that would be unfair to Five. But couldn't we have a white one — or a ginger? We've never had a ginger.'

'Whatever colour it was,' he persisted, 'I couldn't face a Six. The name would stick in my throat. Supposing it got lost, like One used to get lost, and I had to go round the garden calling Six! Six! Six! . . .'

Then, suddenly, the spell was broken, and we both began to laugh. It was rather uncertain, quavery sort of laughter, but at least it was laughter. If you make the experiment of trying to call out 'Six! Six! Six!', you will understand why we laughed. You will find yourself calling something that sounds distinctly inelegant.

'Well, then,' I said at last, 'it will have to be a Seven.'

'It would be a pretty name,' admitted Gaskin, grudgingly.

V

So the wonderful search began — the search for Seven. It took me to private houses and barns and pet-shops and haylofts, and it was only by the sternest resolve and the strictest moral discipline that I managed to stop myself from turning Merry Hall into a vast Cattery, with so many kittens that they filled the cellars and bulged out of the attic windows, as in a Walt Disney cartoon.

At last I found him — the kitten who broke down all resistance. He was in the backyard of an old farm-house near the village of Ladslove, sitting all by himself in a sort of cage made of wire-netting, to keep the spaniels from getting at him. He looked very forlorn and rather frightened; his brothers and sisters had been taken away; and his mother was of a flighty disposition, and was apt to disappear to the woods for days on end, where — it is generally thought — she behaved in a manner which, if she had been a human, would have brought her into conflict with the authorities.

Dusk was just falling, but even in the half-light his coat shone bright ginger, and his baby eyes — I noticed them with a sudden stab of recollection — were as blue as One's had been. He staggered forward with that enchanting, slightly drunken gait which all kittens have. Then he paused, and shrunk back and stared at me. I was very big. He was very small. The world was all very new and alarming, filled with strange scents and sounds, such as the flap, flap, flap of the old sack which covered the opening of the box which till then had been his only home.

He turned towards the sack, flapping in the wind. I realized that this was the moment to prove my quality. So I bent forward and put my hand, very gently, behind the sack, and scratched, turning my forefinger into a mouse. (In these weighty matters, it is important that the scratcher, whether male or female, should *believe* that his or her finger is, in fact, a mouse.) Nobody had ever scratched like that for Seven before. He crouched, in fierce concentration, which was no less effective because his back legs were not quite strong enough to support his behind, which wobbled perilously. Then he made a daring leap forward, of at least six inches. Whereupon I ceased to be a mouse, and became, from that moment, his master, and lifted him up, and put him inside my coat, and he began to purr. It was, I rejoiced to discover, a purr of vintage quality, rich and fruity, with luscious overtones.

I decided that he must be taken home there and then.

Gaskin must be presented, as it were, with a *chat accompli*. If I were to delay, or to enter into discussions, there was no knowing what emotional disturbances might result. And so it was only a few minutes later that Seven was placed in a basket filled with straw and heather, and lifted into the car. To his eternal credit, he never ceased to purr. And off we set together, driving very slowly through the winding lanes, to a life of new adventures.

VI

I suspected that my arrival with a new kitten would lead to high drama. My suspicions were right. It did.

Gaskin did an act. Trying to conceal the obvious fact that he had been swept in by his very first glimpse of Seven, poking his nose through the basket, he protested vigorously. Why had I not telephoned to tell him I was bringing Seven? Nothing was in readiness. No preparations had been made. Nobody had been Warned. (I had a strange sense that I was being reproved for not giving him time to put fresh linen in the bedroom, and a bottle of Vichy water on the bedside table, and a new tablet of Rose Geranium soap on the wash-stand.)

'But, Gaskin, I *had* to bring him straight away. And you must admit that he is heaven.'

I lifted the lid of the basket. Seven sat up and stared around him.

Gaskin, with a supreme effort, averted his eyes from the pink, inquiring nose in the basket.

'What Four and Five will think, I do *not* know. If I had only had a little warning. . . .'

'But they will have to get used to him sooner or later.'

'And where will they all eat?' he demanded remorselessly.

'Four is fussy enough as it is. His plate always has to be put on the floor next to the gas stove. But Five won't eat unless his plate is put on the draining board.'

'Really, the house must be big enough to find some corner for his plate. If necessary he can have the entire dining-room.'

Gaskin ignored this sarcasm. 'He's not big enough to get through the cat-door. He'll have to have a box.'

'Well, it won't be the first time there's been a box. Nor, I hope, the last.'

Gaskin heaved a deep sigh. But his role was becoming more and more difficult to sustain. Seven was exerting all his charm. And at that moment he evidently decided that Gaskin must be finally conquered. For he staggered out of the basket, and advanced unsteadily to the edge of the table. And then he held out his paw.

Gaskin gulped. There was no more to be said. He lifted him up. 'Seven,' he said, softly. 'Well, it's a pretty name.'

CHAPTER VIII

MOVING MOUNTAINS

WE can now return to our box of magic earth — the sponge-bag full of rich, sweet loam that I brought back from the hills of Wales and set down on the poisoned lawn.

If there had been a wizard's wand in the house, it could have been waved over that box until the earth spread over the whole garden. In the absence of a wand, it must be increased by other means. How? Obviously I could not spend my life rushing up to Wales, dangling sponge-bags. The earth would have to come from much nearer afield, and there would have to be a great deal of it.

The question was . . . where was it to be found?

I decided to leave that question, for the moment, unanswered. That there *was* magic earth, somewhere on the horizon, I had no doubt whatever. From my window, on a clear day, you could see the blue outline of a little range that bore the pretty name of Ladslove Hill, and I knew that there were wild rhododendrons growing in the valleys below. So the earth out there must have a quality of magic, and one day I would go there and get it.

In the meantime, I assumed that the earth had already arrived, and I set myself the exciting task of drawing up a grand design as to how to use it. This task was soon accomplished. The whole of the further end of the lawn should be transformed into a vast bank of magic soil, some fifty yards long. On this bank should be planted a succession of glorious rhododendrons; they would glow like coloured bonfires, and they would — I hoped — arouse feelings of the bitterest envy and malice in the bosoms of Miss Emily and Our Rose.

But there was one unpleasant snag to this pleasing plan. No speck of the poisonous chalk, on which the bank would rest, must be allowed to touch the roots of the rhododendrons. How was this to be prevented? By digging a pit deep enough to give the roots room to expand without touching the chalk? No, that would have been useless. In the end, the poison would filter through with the rains, and kill the precious things.

Very well. There was only one solution.

The whole of the ground must be concreted.

I have put this sentence in italics because — well, if *you* suddenly decided that a large portion of your garden would have to be covered in concrete, in order to support a mountain of earth which was not there, in the hope of growing quantities of shrubs which did not, as yet, exist — you might be inclined to put it in italics, too.

You might also be inclined to observe that it was not practical gardening, that it was not, indeed, practical anything at all, that it was a gross example of putting the cart before the horse, etc. etc.

You would be quite right. It *is* an example of putting

the cart before the horse, and that is how I happen to prefer to operate. Carts *should* be put before horses, firmly. It is the only progressive philosophy. If a man goes through life putting horses before carts he deserves to end up in one. There are too many people in the world with this gloomy outlook. They are the sort of people who, when they are furnishing a flat, begin by purchasing all those objects which they regard as necessities, such as beds, chairs and saucepans. This is quite the wrong way of going about it. Surely the first object to be purchased should be a small jade cat, with — if possible — emerald eyes?

'But in that case,' you may protest, 'there would be nothing left for a bed, a chair, or a saucepan.'

To which the only reasonable retort is that if you are so extraordinarily unenterprising as to be unable to procure for yourself a bed, a chair, or a saucepan, there must be something radically wrong with you.

At any rate, I proceeded to concrete a large area of the garden at the end of the lawn. And once again, our peace was disturbed by a period in which we were over-run by those recurrent visitors, The Men. There were Men with picks and shovels, and Men with lorries of sand and gravel, and men with mixers and hose-pipes and loads of bricks, and Gaskin began to show signs of doing another act. 'I did think,' he complained, 'that when we had finished with everything in the house, and when we'd put up the balustrade and dug the water-garden and built the wall, I might have had a few days without a lot of Men tramping into the kitchen asking for cups of tea.'

'They won't be here for ever, Gaskin.'

Gaskin gave a sceptical sniff. 'What I'd like to know is what's going to happen when it's all finished?'

'You'll see.'

It was easy enough to give Gaskin this careless assurance, but there were days when I asked myself the same question — what was going to happen when it was all finished? By an unfortunate miscalculation I seemed to have given the contractors an order to concrete nearly twice as much ground as I had originally intended, and it had already been dug up and prepared before I was able to stop them.

It was all rather alarming. Day by day the garden bore a closer resemblance to the foundations for a municipal town hall. And day by day the bills . . . but we will draw a veil over that.

The only thing that sustained me was the thought of the rhododendrons — those distant bonfires of scarlet and purple, glimmering on the horizon of my imagination. Once the earth had been obtained for them, they could be set in place, and could begin, as it were, to smoulder. So let us dismiss the Men, and send their lorries flying, and leave behind us the stretch of arid concrete, and take a trip to Ladslove Hill.

II

Ladslove Hill was a vast, inexhaustible treasure-trove of peat and leaf-mould and silver sand, blended into a soft dark compost, so sweet and fragrant that you could almost have eaten it. It still is, in spite of the large quantities of it which have been removed to Merry Hall. At the risk of sounding tiresomely repetitive, I must insist that this soil had — for me, at any rate — a quality of magic.

You see, I do believe very firmly that there exists a 'radiation' — for lack of a more explicit word — between the soil and ourselves, and that if this radiation is disturbed we are in some sense incomplete. There are chalk people, and there are sand people, and there are people who have an obvious affinity with heavy, sticky clay. And there are people like myself who demand peat, not merely because they want to grow rhododendrons but because the moment they set foot on it they respond to it physically and emotionally; their perceptions are intensified and they have a sense of well-being which is otherwise inexplicable. This theory of mine might perhaps serve as a modest footnote in the researches of radiaesthesia, whose pioneers are opening up some of the most exciting territories of human thought. It is a theory which throws light on many dark places. As an obvious example I would cite Emily Brontë; I believe that the passionate longing for her Yorkshire moors was not merely a sign of loneliness; it was not a sentimental desire to return to certain familiar sights and sounds; it was something far deeper and more mysterious. The dark heathery earth of Haworth was physically necessary to her, it had the right 'radiation'; when she walked over it she walked in harmony, when she was away from it her soul was sick. Like the heather itself, she needed an acid soil.

So let us pay our visit to Ladslove Hill, that we have only seen, so far, from the bedroom window on a clear day. It lies some fifteen miles from Meadowstream, and one of the strange things about it is that hardly anybody ever goes there. You can wander about for hours, cresting the summits and plunging into the valleys, and you will see not a soul — not a keeper nor a woodman nor a solitary hiker. Sometimes I have a curious feeling that for the great majority of people it must be invisible, that it just isn't there for them. Or that it sends out warning radiations to them, informing them that it does not wish to be visited except by the right people. (In a few moments I shall find myself writing like Our Rose, but I can't help that.)

I wonder if you are one of the people whom Ladslove Hill would have welcomed? I wonder how you would have reacted, if you had been with me on my expeditions, which grew more and more frequent? Would you have had the same sudden lightening of the spirit as the landscape changed from chalk to peat and sand? It happens, as it so often happens in England, in the space of a few yards. At the bottom of the hill you are still on chalk, with the giant thorns, the sour ashes and elders which tolerate that abominable substance; and then, as you begin to climb, everything alters; the soil darkens, and across it dance little groups of silver birches to meet you, like girls in a ballet; the banks grow golden with bracken and glow with heather; groves of giant sweet chestnuts stretch into the distance; the wind is fragrant with the scent of pines. It is a new world . . . and all because of the soil itself, the good earth.

I would park the car, and walk off to a clearing, and sit down on a tree trunk, and stare at that earth. Sometimes I would get down on my knees, and take lumps of it in my hands, and crumble it up, and hold it close to my nose, to savour it more fully. To the casual passer-by this behaviour might appear eccentric, but I cannot understand why people should think one foolish to be excited by the earth from which all life springs and to which all life must return. It was such beautiful stuff. There was history in it . . . a long, dark, stormy history of wind and rain and leaves falling, falling through the years, from distant skies. Maybe there was blood in it, the blood of little woodland creatures who had struggled their last in fierce, forgotten battles. But there was happy history, too . . . a history of sunlight and ripening seeds and the eternal caress of pine needles drifting down. It had a strange purity; you could take it in your hands and let it fall again, and your hands were still quite clean; indeed, they were cleaner, because the earth had left some of its scent on them, and it was the scent of moss and rain and — strangely enough — of snow.

This earth had a positive, and to me, a compelling beauty. Whatever grew from it must be good. Even when the rain was falling I would stay there, and sniff the rain, and watch the water gathering in the little pools. The water in those pools was golden . . . a pale amber shade of gold that seemed to have a special virtue and beneficence. When you leant forward and dipped your hands in it, you felt a sort of blessing; it was so clean, so immaculate, so near to heaven. After all, heaven was the place from which it had just arrived, and here it was at your feet, with all the tiny enchantments of nature around it, heathers and spindles and velvet mosses, and over its pale surface the soft shadow of trembling ferns.

III

I cannot remember the precise moment when I decided to play the role of Mahomet, or rather, the role that he would have liked to play . . . the Mover of Mountains. At first, my trips to Ladslove Hill were simply the result of the compulsion which the soil had for me; I did not connect it with the experiments in my own garden. The concrete was being laid down, and in due course the right earth would be laid on top of it. This earth would, presumably, arrive from somewhere or other in lorries, at vast expense. It did not occur to me, as I ranged the hill, that here was the earth I was seeking, and that all I had to do was to take it home.

I fancy that the Mahomet role was thrust upon me by slow degrees. As my trips to Ladslove Hill became more

K   145

frequent, I developed the habit of digging up clumps of wild heather to plant on the bank near the orchard, and with each clump of heather there had to be enough earth to protect it from the limy soil in which it would be planted.[1] Little by little the clumps of heather grew in size, and so did the earth which went with them, till one day the whole boot of the car was packed tight. That must have been the day when I definitely decided about being Mahomet. For it was then that I realized that if the boot could be filled with earth, so could the whole car. And if the car could be filled once, it could be filled fifty times . . . five thousand times.

Life suddenly assumed a wild and almost alarming excitement. I saw myself embarking on an endless succession of enchanted journeys, careering up the hill in an empty car, rushing backwards and forwards with armfuls of this glorious substance, and then careering home again. No — not careering. One would have to be rather slow and stately, because the car would be decidedly top-heavy.

I decided that the best way to get the most earth in the car would be to put a sheet over the back seat, so when I got home I went in to see Gaskin, as I always do in moments of crisis.

'Gaskin, have we got such a thing as an old sheet in the house?'

'We've got my ironing sheet,' replied Gaskin.

'May I have it, please?'

Gaskin, not unnaturally, replied that he needed it himself.

'Surely you can find another one somewhere?'

There were only linen sheets, said Gaskin. To use a linen

---

[1] The only heathers which tolerate lime are the winter-flowering varieties, *erica carnea*, and one summer variety, the *mediterranea*.

sheet for the ironing board would be, in his opinion, 'a sin'.
'Very well. I'll borrow it for tomorrow afternoon.'
'What do you want it for?'

It was a simple question, and it was a simple situation, but for some reason it was difficult to answer. How do you explain, to an ordinary, sensible person, that you need a sheet in order to put it at the back of the car and pile earth on it? And that you need it urgently and desperately? And that this is the most important thing in life for you? And that you must do it, and continue to do it, again and again? And that if you are prevented from doing it you will go, slowly but firmly, into a decline?

However, in the end I got my sheet, and was able to embark on this folly of all follies without too much protest. As far as Gaskin was concerned it had one great advantage. It might ruin my suits, it might transform my car into a replica of a station manure wagon, and it might — and almost certainly would — involve me in conflict with Authority. But it would not call for a new eruption of Men.

So there we were. The scene was set . . . a very simple scene, but a very thrilling one. In the foreground, a bleak stretch of concrete. (But you must not forget that ghostly lights from unborn rhododendrons were flickering over it.) In the background, the enchanted hill. Panting at the door, a small saloon car, with a dust sheet over the back seat, and a lot of sacking in the boot. Seated at the wheel of the car an author, gently patting the straws in his hair, and feeling that life is quite exceptionally worth living.

Off we go, over the hills and far away. We leave the car in a deserted clearing, and creep out, with a sheet and a spade, and down a heathery path, till we find a dark, fragrant patch of earth. Then we lay down the sheet, and drive in the spade, and lift out a glorious lump and deposit it on the sheet. When we have enough we twist up the sheet, and swing the bundle over our back, and totter back to the car and empty it in . . . dreaming all the time of the ghostly purple bonfires that will one day arise from these strange endeavours.

I think that I was never happier than on these earth-gathering expeditions. They held nearly everything that makes life, for me, worth living. I could never decide whether they are better alone or in company. When one was alone there was a faint spice of danger . . . the woods were so thick and so silent, and one felt so remote, delving down among the roots of the wild rhododendrons, and staggering back with a load that almost broke one's back. Sometimes I wondered what would happen if one tripped over a root and fell, and were suffocated under a gigantic pile of acid soil? What would the *Evening News* make of it?

AUTHOR'S MYSTERIOUS DEATH

THE CHARRED SHEET

MYSTERY WOMAN AT THE YARD

That would be one way of looking at it. The more intellectual organs might have a different approach . . . if they took any notice at all, which is improbable. They would hint at obscure complexes. They would find Oedipus lurking coyly in the leaf-mould, and what they would make of the sheet is nobody's business.

Why worry? I have never understood this strange prejudice against complexes. I am a mass of complexes, and so are you, and I am quite devoted to them. The more. the merrier, as far as I am concerned.

Now this is a true story. Therefore, like many true stories, it must end in what may perhaps seem an anti-climax. It would have been nice to have drawn a final picture of myself standing on a mountain of earth with folded arms, staring haughtily at an admiring group of Miss Emily, Our Rose, Marius and all the rest of them, and proclaiming . . . 'I did it with my little spade.'

It was not quite like that. True, I did cover quite a sizeable stretch of concrete with the magic soil — enough, that is to say, for the cats to decide that I had done it for their special benefit, in order to provide them with the most luxurious facilities for powdering their noses. But you would be surprised, you really would, to know how many times you have to fill a small saloon car with earth in order to create a mound, let alone a mountain.

And the weeks were slipping by, and a nip was coming into the air, and Nature was busy with her paint-brush of a night-time, spreading the first coat of gold on the maples, and flecking the liquid ambers with crimson lake.

So with a sigh of reluctance but also of relief, I decided that my earth, my special self-gathered earth, should act as a magic foundation, and that the rest would have to be imported in a more prosaic way, by lorry, from firms who dealt in that sort of thing. Making this decision was like stepping out of fairyland into Fleet Street. However, it had to be made.

So we end as we began. With lorries, churning up the drive, and vast expense, and Men, drinking Gaskin's tea.

But my earth must have spread its magic through the whole of the imported soil. For the rhododendrons have flourished like the green bay tree, and every spring the bonfires smoulder and glow deeper and break into flames of purple and mauve and scarlet. They are so beautiful that I often take out a chair and sit in front of them, and project myself spiritually inside them. (See previous passages on the Art of Shrinking.) The world looks quite different if you view it, calmly and objectively, from the shelter of a large rhododendron blossom, with a sort of scarlet tent over your head, and a speckled rug under your feet . . . though it is rather alarming when bumble-bees, the size of bullocks, peer in at the entrance, and buzz like sirens. However, in order to experience these delights you must have an acid soil. And that, as by now you may have gathered, takes some getting.

CHAPTER IX

MIXED BUNCH

I N this chapter we are going for a walk with Marius, and when we return, Our Rose and Miss Emily are coming to tea, when Four will behave in a most outrageous fashion. It will be generally agreed that no author, in the space of a single chapter, can be expected to pack more thrills, more suspense, and more general instruction.

But seriously — if the word is not inapposite — these small events did happen to occur on the same day in my life, and they are the sort of events which, to me, are more exciting than the headlines in the daily papers. Some people find importance in the photographs of those titanic mushrooms of atomic poison which are periodically exploded over the world's deserts; I find greater importance in one very small mushroom which mysteriously springs up in the shadow of the tool-shed. This is not being smug, though you might think it. The titanic poisonous mushroom is an example of the meanness and folly of man; the very small tool-shed mushroom is an example of the bounty and wisdom of God. It is better to contemplate the latter. Otherwise one might as well go and jump over the white cliffs of Dover which, being composed of that noxious substance, chalk, are a suitable place for such melancholy exits from the world.

Apart from these philosophical reflections, it is high time that Marius and Our Rose and Miss Emily stepped into the picture again.

In the last chapter, when we were collecting earth on Ladslove Hill, I made myself rather the star character, and you may have gained the impression that I moved my mountain singlehanded, staggering about with gigantic bundles on my back, in solitary state. This was not the case. As often as not, Marius would accompany me, and in spite of his pallor, his elegant stoop, and his general air of Foreign Office fragility, he was much the stronger partner. Indeed, when the spade was in his hands, sending the magic earth flying on to the sheet, I had often to stop him. He might be a Samson, I would remind him, but I was not. Besides, there was a horrid thing called rupture, which seemed to be very much in vogue among middle-aged authors. (Graham Greene, one often suspects, was born with it.) So Marius would stop, with reluctance, and sometimes — in an absent-minded way — he would lift the whole load of Sisyphus on to his own back, and stroll back to the car with as little concern as if he were taking a constitutional in St. James's Park.

And afterwards, when the car was packed to capacity, he would usually indicate that he would like to take a walk before going home — 'to stretch the limbs' — as if they were not stretched enough already. It is one of these walks that I wish to celebrate, because, as we set out, I suggested that we might pick a bunch of wild flowers for Our Rose, who was coming to tea.

II

'A bunch for Our Rose?' Marius nodded. 'That,' he said mysteriously, 'might provide some quiet entertainment.'

I could not imagine what he meant, and for the moment I forgot about it. We were both relaxed and happy, and disinclined to talk, and we drifted our separate ways in search of flowers, calling to each other from time to time over our shoulders. I had found some very pretty silver maple leaves, which looked enchanting against a few sprays of Queen Anne's Lace. I dreaded to think what Our Rose might do with them. She always made me think of the Queen in Alice . . . Chop Off Their Heads was her theme song. I decided that my bunch should be largely composed of leaves and ferns, and I also decided that I should not give it to Our Rose at all.

It must have been nearly an hour later that I saw Marius climbing up the path from the valley. As he came up to me I saw that he was holding a small bunch of flowers which, frankly, did not strike me as very pretty. There were merely some campions, of a sickly shade of pink, and a few white daises. By the side of the daises was a solitary specimen of that curious, rather sinister plant that grows in deep shadow — 'the long purple'.

He paused, and held the flowers at arm's length. 'And now,' he said, 'we only need some nettles.'

'Why nettles, Marius?'

He blinked at me in surprise. 'Surely you see the allusion?' Then, since he observed that he was, as usual, a step ahead, he added: 'These were the flowers which poor Ophelia wove into her wreath before she "fell in the weeping brook".'

I stared at the bunch. The strange, sad words of the Queen echoed in my memory:

There is a willow grows aslant the brook
That shows his hoar leaves in the glassy stream;
Therewith fantastic garlands did she make
Of crowflowers, nettles, daises, and long purples. . . .

'So these are crowflowers?' I pointed to the campions.
'Yes. They are, of course, a species of lychnis, and in Shakespeare's time they were used to symbolize a fair maiden. In fact, the whole wreath is full of the most powerful symbolism. The daisy — the "day's eye" — is a token of virginity. This virginity has been stung and outraged by the nettles. Over it all is the deadly shadow of the long purples. You remember how the Queen described them?

Long purples
That liberal shepherds give a grosser name
But our cold maids do dead men's fingers
call them.

'In the whole of literature,' he went on, 'I doubt whether there is a line so evocative. "*Crowflowers, nettles, daises, and long purples.*" Nothing could be simpler. But one trembles to think what Freud would have made of it.' He gave a faint shudder, bent down, and laid the little bunch in the shadow of a hedge. 'I had been thinking of giving these flowers to Our Rose, but I feel that I should be ill-advised to do so, for it is just conceivable that she might recognize their significance. It would be intolerable if she decided to add the role of Ophelia to her many impersonations.'

We walked on for a little while in silence. We were skirting the edge of a beech wood, which . . . like all beech woods . . . was pretending to be a cathedral. I thought how pleasant it was, strolling along like this with a companion

Afternoon

such as Marius, who seemed to recall a story in every shadow and a legend in every leaf.

At length I asked him: 'If you *were* making a bunch for Rose — a really suitable bunch, I mean, which would express her character, what would you choose?'

'I should certainly include a spray of clematis.'

'Why?'

'Because Rose is of all creatures the most artificial, and . . . as I need not remind you . . . the clematis is the symbol of artifice. In the time of Nero its stains were used by the beggars in the streets of Rome to produce artificial ulcers on their skin. By the side of the clematis I should place a few leaves of sycamore.'

'Why sycamore?'

He shook his head at me. 'I often think that you ask these elementary questions merely from a desire to expose me in some inaccuracy.'

'I assure you, Marius, that I do nothing of the sort. I have never pretended to be a scholar. . . .'

'This is not a question of scholarship,' he interrupted, with some severity. 'Unless it is a sign of scholarship to have read the New Testament. Which, no doubt, will soon be the case, unless . . .' He broke off abruptly, and took my arm. 'But perhaps I am being unfair. I have such an affection for old wives' tales that I sometimes persuade myself that everybody else must share it.'

'What is the old wives' tale about the sycamore?'

'It centres round Zaccheus, the publican.'

'At least I have heard of *him*.'

'He was one of the crowd on the day that Christ made his triumphal entry into Jerusalem. To get a better view, he climbed into a sycamore tree. So the sycamore tree has become a symbol of curiosity.'

'As simple as that!' I could not help smiling at the aptness of Marius's choice for Our Rose. Artifice carried to absurdity . . . insatiable curiosity.

'But she has her pleasanter qualities, too,' I suggested.

'Agreed; that is why we should include some wallflowers.'

'Wouldn't she regard that as faintly insulting?'

'If she chose the Victorian interpretation, no doubt she would. But if she had not forgotten all that she learned at school . . .' here he cast me a glance that I can only describe as affectionately malicious . . . 'she might cast her mind back to the days of the last of the troubadours. They wore bunches of wallflowers as they sang their way from castle to castle. Why? Because the wallflower is a symbol of fidelity in misfortune. All around them the castles were falling, the abbeys were sinking into disrepair. But the wallflowers stayed on, blooming as gaily as ever in the crumbling walls . . . as they bloom to this day, in some of the remnants of our stately homes.' He sighed. 'If one were a poet, there might be a few lines to be written on such a theme. The wandering minstrels . . . the sunlight fading on the turrets . . . the scent of the dark velvety flowers . . . the music drifting up to the medieval skies . . . the birth of a legend. Fidelity in spite of misfortune; faith in the face of disaster.'

'Yes,' I said. 'I think that Rose should be happy about her wallflowers.' I was recalling all sorts of little anonymous acts of kindness which could be laid to her credit.

I had been so fascinated by Marius's conversation that I was surprised to see that we had already come to the car. For once in a way, I was reluctant to go. However, Rose and Emily were coming to tea, and I had promised to drop Marius at his house on the way back. So we climbed in, and, after the usual preliminaries of pressing down the piled-up soil so that too much of it did not fall down our necks, we began to trundle home. From time to time Marius, as we drove, added an imaginary flower to Our Rose's bunch. There was, I remember, a piece of mignonette. She might not have been too pleased with that, for its traditional meaning is 'Your qualities surpass your charms'. However, perhaps she would have been appeased by his spray of angelica, which symbolizes 'inspiration'.

'If we still felt that we had not done her justice,' concluded Marius as I dropped him at his gate, 'we could always give her a pineapple. And I hope that you have, at least, some faint conception of the significance of *that*!'

For once in a way, he was right.

III

Needless to say, I did not give Marius's bunch, with its Freudian connotations, to Our Rose. It would have been embarrassing if she had interpreted it correctly. Nor did I give her my own bunch. It was far too pretty and too delicate.

Indeed, for the time being, I forgot about bunches altogether. For as soon as I got home, I found to my dismay that this was one of the afternoons when Four had decided to play his dramatic role of The Maltreated Cat. And since Four was a particular favourite with Miss Emily, no moment could have been less opportune.

I realized what 'Four' was up to as soon as I walked into the cloakroom to wash the earth off my hands. 'Four' usually follows in order to assist in these ablutions by springing on to the edge of the basin, and dabbing at the water with a soft black paw. But today, as soon as I turned on the water, Four — who was sitting in the doorway — registered horror and dismay, and crept out of sight as though he had suddenly seen some fearful fiend. It was too tiresome. He had decided to play his role — The Maltreated Cat.

A word must be said in explanation of this singular performance. It is a part of the deepest poignancy, it wrings the hearts of all who are privileged to see it, and it never fails to convince them that Four's master is a secret Cat Beater of the most diabolical variety.

However, it really has nothing to do with me; it is forced upon Four by Five, at intervals of about once a month. At heart, the two are deeply devoted; they sleep together every night, with their arms round one another's necks, a purring duet in beige and black. But now and then Five decides to assert his authority. Why he should do this is anybody's guess; maybe it is because he suddenly remembers that he is an alley cat, whereas Four — or the black fifty per cent of him — is of royal Siamese descent. Whatever the reason, the procedure is always the same. In the middle of a game, or at the end of a walk, or even when they are merely conversing quietly by the fireside, Five suddenly gives Four a tremendous clout across the ear. Just like that, out of the blue. And Four, instead of retaliating, as would be well within his power, accepts it meekly, and slinks away, with tragedy written all over him, from his sad green eyes to his black drooping tail. For the rest of the day or the night he is usually to be encountered under a sofa in the music room, sighing, and studying his role of The Maltreated Cat, which he proceeds to play for the next two days. One would have thought that, by now, he would have known it by heart.

Yes, we *have* spoken to Five about it. We have spoken at length, and with great severity. We have lifted him on to the kitchen table, and folded our arms, and stared at him, and asked him, in the coldest of tones: '*Why* do you behave like this to poor Four? What has he done? Do you not

realize that you are giving him an inferiority complex?'
All we receive, in answer to these not unreasonable questions, is a cold, unflinching stare from Five's beautiful green eyes. Sometimes, in desperation, we have given Five a token slap. It has absolutely no effect on Five; it does not even make him blush; but the effect on ourselves is devastating. We *are* Cat Beaters, we must rush to the cupboard and open a tin of something extra special to show that we did not really mean it. But then, we think — with the tinopener poised in our hands — we *did* mean it, because it was for Four whom we were really fighting. By now we are in an emotional maelstrom, torn this way and that, not knowing what to do, nor where to look, and we only wish that instead of cats we had collected groups of Staffordshire cows, who would stay quietly on the mantelpiece, and make no demands on us except an occasional flick of the duster.

Meanwhile, Five sits and stares. And Four remains under the sofa, sighing deeply, and studying his role. The role of The Maltreated Cat.

IV

It was, as we have said, on such an afternoon that Miss Emily and Our Rose came to tea. They had proposed themselves together the day before, to my great satisfaction, because I had heard rumours that their relations were more than usually strained.

This visit suggested that the rumours had no foundation. However, as soon as they began to talk, I wondered if, after all, relations were so harmonious.

The conversation opened with a skirmish around the big mixed bunch of flowers which always stands behind the piano against the white screen in the music room. As soon as she saw it, Our Rose stepped forward and stood in front of it, clasping her hands in apparent ecstasy.

'There, Emily! What did I tell you? I knew!'

Miss Emily merely sniffed.

Our Rose turned to me. 'I saw it! I saw every petal of it, as we were coming down the lane!' Noticing my look of surprise, she pointed to her forehead. 'I saw it here, in my brain. Didn't I, Emily? Didn't I describe it all to you, only ten minutes ago?'

'You said that there would probably be lilies,' returned Miss Emily, tersely. 'Which is hardly surprising.'

'Oh come, darling, there was a great deal more than that! What about the copper beech?'

'Mr. Nichols often uses copper beech.'

'And the polyantha roses? Didn't I even show you how they would droop over the edge of the vase? Didn't I *trace* them for you?'

'You waved your hands about a great deal, my dear. But that is nothing unusual.'

Our Rose gave an artificial laugh. 'Dear Emily finds it difficult to accept these things,' she said. 'I suppose it is only natural, if one has not the gift.'

Miss Emily tossed her head. 'If it is a gift for knowing precisely what one is going to see in other people's homes, it is a gift I could very well do without. It would make life very dull. Like knowing what one was going to have for dinner.'

'Oh no, dear! Not at all like that. Quite a different plane. Let me try to show you. You see, it's like this. Here is a Brain.' She made a gesture towards me, at the same time sketching an oval in the air, which made me feel like a sort of educated egg, floating in space. 'The Brain is creating beauty, and so it sends out Vibrations. If one is on the same plane as those Vibrations' . . . she smiled modestly, to indicate that she was on such a plane . . . 'one tunes in to them. All quite simple dear, when one comes to think of it. Like asking for a number on the telephone, and getting it.'

'If it were the Meadowstream exchange,' retorted Miss Emily, 'it might not be so simple as all that.'

Rose refused to be dragged down to the common level. She ignored Miss Emily, and stepped nearer to the vase. 'Quite, quite extraordinary!' she murmured. 'Every leaf, every petal, exactly as I knew it would be! It would be almost frightening if it were not so wonderful.' A thought struck her. 'I wonder if it would work both ways?'

'How do you mean?'

'I wonder if *you* might one day sense what I was doing? If you might suddenly see one of my pictures, as it were, floating before you?'

This was really too much. I knew, only too well, what Rose would be doing, all through the floral year. She would be chopping off the heads of irises and sticking them on to pinholders in the shape of a fan. She would be contriving repulsive little water-gardens, with oldy worldy gnomeys sitting on the edge; she would be pushing pom-pom dahlias up behinds of china fox-terriers. If these horrors were to come drifting towards me through the ether, at all times of the day and night, life would be insupportable.

Fortunately I was saved from any need to comment on Rose's flights of fancy, for at this moment Four came upon the scene.

I had hoped against hope that Four, if he decided to visit us, would have thought better about playing his role of The Maltreated Cat. He was very fond of ladies, and they might cheer him up. However, his intentions were all too clear from the moment he arrived.

He appeared in the doorway, drooping in an attitude of intense dejection. Although he had eaten the major portion of two large whiting that morning, a leg of rabbit and various other oddments, he managed to convey a subtle suggestion of extreme malnutrition.

He stared round the room in what might be described as 'a wild surmise', caught my eye, registered terror, and shot under the sofa. It was too tiresome.

'Dear me!' exclaimed Miss Emily, who never misses anything. 'Whatever can be the matter with poor Four?'

I went over to the sofa. 'It's just an act.'

As though to contradict this assertion, Four popped his head out, cast an agonized glance at the ceiling, as though demanding to be saved from his brutal master, and then shot back again.

'The poor little thing looks quite terrified,' said Miss Emily.

'Perhaps he's been frightened by some dog', I suggested, rather feebly. It would have been far too complicated to explain Four's relations with Five.

'Oh no!' It was Rose who spoke. She had risen from her chair, and was standing behind, just behind me. 'Not a dog. No *dog* could have done that.'

'Done what?' I demanded, rather shortly. It was only a little while ago that Rose had pretended to be terrified of all cats, and to swoon when they came near her. And here she was, with no sign of swooning, laying down the law about Four.

'Done what?' I repeated.

'It is not so much what has been *done*,' proclaimed Rose, 'as the spirit in which it has been done.'

'More vibrations?' snorted Miss Emily.

'If you must know, dear, yes. I can tell. I *know*. If I could put my hand on him for a moment. . . .'

163

'I'll get him out,' I said.

It was a very tense moment. There, behind me, was Miss Emily, on whom Four's performance had evidently made a deep effect. By her stood Our Rose, determined to be psychic, to show off her precious Vibrations. I only hoped that Four would be sensible and relax.

I knelt down, stretched my hand under the sofa, and caught hold of him. He immediately went rigid. Had I been alone, needless to say, I should have left him in peace; when a cat goes rigid it is both kindness and common sense to leave it to itself. But I was not alone, so I held on, and pulled him towards me, as gently as possible. Four resisted every inch of the way, digging his claws into the carpet. I was reminded of a bloodthirsty print which used to hang in my nursery. It was called 'The R— of the Sabines'. A pious nanny had once unscrewed the frame and scraped out the last three letters of the word 'Rape', leaving the letter R. In the foreground of this picture a bearded giant was portrayed, dragging a small, dark maiden out of a cave by the hair of her head. That was just how I felt, and now I came to think of it, the small dark maiden had quite a look of Four about her.

At last he was out. I gave him a slow, soft stroke. He cringed from it, as though his entire life had been spent under the lash. He had evidently decided that this was to be the performance of his life.

'May I?'

It was Rose. She had knelt down beside me, with a great rattle of moonstones from her necklace, and was edging me to one side.

'Just an experiment,' she murmured. 'Quite simple.'

I let go of Four. Very slowly Rose stretched out her hand. I prayed that Four might realize that this was a moment when he should bring his role to a climax, when there should be a cringe to end all cringes, and possibly a frenzied struggle to regain the shelter of the sofa. But the Devil had entered into Four. He suddenly ceased to cringe; instead, he raised his head, and opened his eyes wide, and gazed at Rose as though she were an angel of deliverance.

It was the moonstone necklace, of course, dangling in front of him. When human beings dangled things in front of him, he knew that it was a signal to play. And when there was a signal to play, all else was forgotten.

'You see?' breathed Rose, with maddening complacency. 'It's just a question of trust.'

'It's a question of moonstones,' I retorted. If only Four would give a sharp dab at her neck! And indeed, it looked as though he might do so, for he began to push out a tentative paw.

'Complete and absolute *trust*,' repeated Rose, in dreamy tones. 'Emily, dear, come and look!'

Miss Emily came over. 'You see?' continued Rose. 'The little darling is stretching out his little paw. He wants to shake hands!'

Although Miss Emily made no reply but a sniff, she was obviously impressed. Four's eyes were riveted on the necklace, and he was preparing to make a dab. I knew all the signs.

Half closing her eyes, Rose continued to stroke Four's head in a most unprofessional manner. Four likes to be stroked with great firmness under the chin in an upward direction; Rose was merely flicking her silly scarlet nails over his ears. In normal circumstances he would have despised such attentions, but the necklace hypnotized him.

Then, without warning, Four dabbed. It was a sharp and accurate dab, right at the central stone of the necklace, and if Rose had known anything at all about cats, she would, of course, have been delighted, and encouraged more dabs, and wobbled the necklace about, and eventually taken it off and dragged it over the carpet for Four's delectation. That was the way in which Four had been trained to expect humans to behave, in the matter of necklaces, wrist-watches, neck-ties, dressing-gown cords and suchlike.

However, she did not know anything about cats, and Four's dab gave her such a shock that she toppled off her heels on to the floor. Four, astonished by this unorthodox behaviour, drew back swiftly under the sofa, and resumed the study of his role.

'You've frightened him,' scolded Emily, as I helped Rose to her feet.

'Not at all,' retorted Rose, somewhat breathlessly.

'He only wanted to play,' I said.

Rose shook her head. 'No. It was a gesture. A gesture of trust.'

'It looked to *me* as if he was going to scratch,' snapped Emily.

'Yes, dear. I'm sure it did. And I expect if it had been you, you *would* have been scratched.'

'And may I ask why he should scratch me and not you?'

'Yes, dear, you may. But I doubt if I could tell you.'

'If you're so certain that he won't scratch you, why not put your hand under the sofa and see?'

Rose sighed deeply. 'No, dear, not for a little while, if you don't mind. Later perhaps. These things rather take it out of one.' She sank heavily into a chair.

Miss Emily glared at her. 'Really, my dear, if you are exhausted by merely stroking a cat. . . .'

Rose held up her hand. 'No, dear. It was not a question of merely stroking a cat.'

'Then what was it?'

'It was a question of *giving* something of oneself. So difficult to explain. She smiled wanly in my direction. 'We're always giving, aren't we?' And then, as though to show that the subject was closed . . . 'May we go out and refresh ourselves with the Nerines?'

I was all for going out and 'refreshing ourselves with the Nerines'. (The phrase sounds like going to a bottle party with a lot of negroes; in fact, Rose meant that she wanted to have a look at my pink lilies, which were just coming into flower on the South wall.)

So out we trailed, for Nerine refreshment, leaving Four under the sofa. He must have been feeling the glowing satisfaction of an artist who has given a great performance.

On the way out we met Five, entering the little conservatory. His tail was frizzy and there was a predatory look in his eye. If he were allowed indoors, he would discover Four, and give him another clout, and that might mean that Four would go on playing his role for a whole week. The thought was intolerable. I clapped my hands sharply. 'Five' took the hint, turned tail, and sped across the lawn.

The ladies said nothing, but they exchanged glances. Henceforth, no doubt, I am registered in their minds as an inveterate Cat Beater.

However, perhaps not. For the Nerines were infinitely refreshing, particularly as Rose informed me that all hers had been eaten by mice. There was probably a moral in that, somewhere, but I was too tired to discover it.

CHAPTER X

FOLLY

I T seems a long time since the day when we made that crazy journey to the old house in Hampshire, and returned — as it were — with a balustrade in our pockets. As I look back to the record of that adventure, it seems that you have never really seen the balustrade completed. We left it in chaos, a mountain of stone tumbled haphazard on to the lawn.

Now that it is finished, with the roses clambering over it, perhaps you would spare a moment to glance at it, for it dictates the plan of the whole garden.

It is disposed, on two levels, round the lily pool, which is fifty feet long by eight feet wide, and is shaped like this.

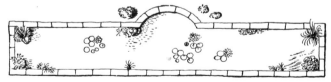

I designed this pool by sticking bamboos into the lawn, joined with pieces of tape, to the great delectation of Four,

Five and Seven, who had their own ideas as to the shape it should take. It has irises and bulrushes in the corners, and five sorts of water-lilies, and lots of goldfish and a dolphin, and a rather angry looking stone crane, sitting on the edge. The crane was put there for two reasons, aesthetic and preventative. The idea was that he would not only look elegant and alluring, but would prevent the onslaughts of a real crane, which has a habit of swooping out of the grey skies of March, very early in the morning, and being beastly to the fish. The idea has proved barren. The real crane is not deterred by the stone one; on the contrary; it has developed a sort of morbid passion for it. I have often looked out of my bedroom window, at dawn, and seen the strangest pecks, and flutterings, and goings-on.

Back to the balustrade.

The designing of this proved far more arduous than the designing of the pool, largely because it had to be done in close conjunction with those perennial invaders, the Men. When the pool was being planned, the only really serious distractions were occasioned by Four, Five and Seven, who could be shooed away. But you could not shoo away the Men. You needed them to carry gigantic blocks of stone. Even if you did shoo them away, they would only troop off to the kitchen, and stay there drinking Gaskin's tea at about a guinea an hour. One wonders how balustrades ever get erected at all.

At last it was erected, after a great expenditure of physical energy by the Men and an even greater expenditure of nervous energy by myself. I felt like an Egyptian potentate supervising the building of the Pyramids . . . but with a subtle difference . . . I really was concerned lest the Men should overtax their strength. That is the worst of having such a sweet nature. It was rather as though Tut-ankh-

Amen, during the construction of the Pyramids, had bustled round imploring his slaves not to rupture themselves.

So here is the bare outline of the balustrade to date. The operative phrase is *to date*, for this chapter tells the story of yet another Folly, and after a few pages the whole thing will look quite different. Then, and not till then, we will have a beautiful picture of the finished article, drawn by Willie McLaren, the artist who makes these books so much easier to read by his enchanting drawings.

And now I would like you to meet Willie himself, not only because he is well worth meeting, but because it was largely through his encouragement that the Folly came into being.

II

Willie McLaren is very small, very much a Scot, and so utterly absorbed by the excitement of being an artist that even when he goes for a walk over the fields you have the feeling that his footsteps are tracing an intricate design. That is perhaps the reason why, when you go for a walk with Willie, you seldom reach the place you were aiming at. Willie's fingers are incapable of drawing an ugly line; even when he writes a postcard, at top speed, he produces an exquisite eighteenth-century script, with perhaps a garland, or a scroll, or even a cherub, hovering over the address . . . to the occasional confusion of the postman. Incidentally, Willie has some aesthetic theories that are quite enthralling. He believes — if I am not misquoting him — that the standards of Beauty are fixed, eternal and capable of scientific demonstration . . . that there is a sort of divine *geometry* of art to whose immutable laws all the great masterpieces conform, and that the working of these laws can be proved, to an infinite fraction of an inch, in — let us say — the smallest fold of drapery in a fresco by Giotto. I was therefore more than somewhat gratified when Willie, after pacing up and down my balustrade and making a mass of calculations in his notebook, with acute angles and right-angles crossing and re-crossing, turned to me and said: 'As far as it goes it is perfect. It conforms exactly with the lines of the water-garden. The spacing of the steps is precisely as it should be. And the whole thing is right with the lie of the land.'

This was high praise. I was evidently in accord with the Divine Geometrician, which was very consoling. But what did Willie mean by 'as far as it goes'?

'I just feel that it isn't complete,' said Willie.

'So do I. What do you suggest?'

'That's up to you. It's your design.'

I took a deep breath. I knew what I wanted but I was afraid that Willie might disapprove, or even laugh. I wanted pillars, a semi-circle of nice Doric pillars. But nice Doric pillars — N.D.P.s — were even more socially ambitious than N.B.s. Whereas N.B.s suggested stately homes, N.D.P.s implied palaces, and if I spent the rest of my life wandering about in the shadow of N.D.P.s I should almost certainly develop delusions of grandeur.

Another deep breath. Then I said to Willie: 'I should like some Doric pillars. About eight — just here — in a semi-circle.'

To my great relief Willie nodded. 'So would I.'

'I thought you might think the idea absurd.'

'Why? They would be just right.'

'I believe they would. There's only one thing that worries me . . . what would they be for?'

Willie looked at me in surprise. 'Does that matter?'

'I don't know. Most people would say they ought to be

for something.' I was thinking, needless to say, of Miss Emily and Our Rose, who would have a great many pointed questions to ask about the reason for the sudden appearance of a lot of N.D.P.s.

'Then most people,' retorted Willie, 'are idiots. Why should they be *for* anything, if they look beautiful? Of course, you could put a pediment round the top of them, but it would cost a lot of money, and would be rather pointless, in my opinion — for what it's worth.'

'Your opinion, my dear Willie, is worth a great deal.'

'Thank you. If you want an excuse for them, you can just say that they're a Folly.'

'Another?'

'With a capital F. Like the gentlemen of the eighteenth century, when they built reproductions of Greek temples in their parks.' He frowned for a moment, in concentration. 'There's a lot of significance in that capital F, when you come to think of it. Our ancestors gave it to Folly, because they thought Folly was important. We haven't the courage to do that any longer. Do you see what I mean?'

I did, vaguely. And I was quite certain that Willie was right. But there was no time for talk, with Folly jingling her magic bells in the scented air, and N.D.P.s rearing their spectral heads all around us. I must be off, once again, to Mr. Crowther.

III

Mr. Crowther's establishment, when I arrived, was in a state of some confusion. Mr. Crowther had recently purchased from a stately home a pair of immense iron gates, which had only just been set up; indeed, several of the workmen who had transported them were still sitting about in attitudes of near prostration. The gates were flanked by square stone columns, thirty feet high, surmounted by exquisitely carved heraldic animals. There was also a small mountain of shields, scrolls, and devices, still to be filled in.

The arrival of this major architectural monument, which must have disrupted the traffic for some miles, had not perturbed Mr. Crowther at all.

Taking a puff at his cigar, he stared up at the gates and said: 'Now those would be very nice gates, Mr. Beverley, if you had room for them.'

'Yes, they would, Mr. Crowther.' I did not smile, because I had learned that Mr. Crowther, when he makes a statement, means it literally. He did actually mean that they would be very nice gates, Mr. Beverley, if I had room for them. He was not being sarcastic. Mr. Crowther pays one the compliment — and it is a most highly civilized compliment — of assuming that all men are millionaires.

'The person who buys those gates,' proclaimed Mr. Crowther, 'is to be envied.'

Which was, of course, a point of view.

'I suppose somebody *will* buy them?'

He shrugged his shoulders. 'I expect so. One of these days. Somebody usually Turns Up.' He was the complete Mr. Micawber, at that moment. 'Yes, somebody is sure to Turn Up, one of these days. In the meantime I find them very pleasing to contemplate. And now, what can I do for you?'

'I wondered if — by any chance — you had any Doric pillars?'

'I have hundreds. What were they for? A colonnade? A gallery? A temple?'

'Nothing quite so ambitious. One might call it a Folly.'

'Ah yes! Very agreeable. Let us go and look at them.'

We walked through a labyrinth of winding paths, flanked

with statues, urns, broken columns, cherubs, leaden water tanks and heaven knows what else, and emerged into a yard that was piled high with N.D.P.s. They were about nine feet high and most delicately carved. They were precisely what I wanted, except that they were made of wood. True, they had weathered to a very lovely shade of stone grey, but they were wood.

'They are beautiful, Mr. Crowther, but I had been thinking of stone pillars.'

He shook his head. 'I would not advise that. Stone pillars would be three times as expensive and far more trouble to erect.'

'But will these last?'

He gave me a tolerant smile. 'They have lasted already for a hundred and fifty years. I think they should see you out.'

'What is their history?'

He rubbed his hands together. 'Now, there's a little piece of romance for you, Mr. Beverley. They came from Dover. A nice old Regency crescent, facing the sea. The houses were so knocked about during the war that they had to be pulled down, but they saved some bits and pieces — railings, and doors, and bow-windows, and fan-lights and that sort of thing. And these pillars, which I bought.'

He took me by the arm. 'Come over here, and I'll show you something.'

He led me to a pile of pillars that had been stacked at a short distance from the others. 'These are slightly damaged,' he said. 'Nothing much, but some people are fussy. Look! See that?'

He pointed to a scar in the wood — a gash about two inches long.

'Do you know what that is? That is the mark of shrapnel!'

I stared at the scar . . . as I have so often stared, since that day.

'And here is another. You could have them filled in, of course,' he went on, 'but I myself should leave them. To me, they have romance. Do you agree?'

I did indeed. We stood there for a while, saying little, running our hands over the pale, stone-like wood. If only those pillars could have spoken! For a hundred and fifty years they had stood facing the iron-grey sea of the English Channel — facing France, and Europe. They had withstood not only the slings and arrows of the elements, the lash of the rain and the sting of the spray, but the sterner assaults of history. In their shadows had lurked the refugees from many wars; soldiers had marched by them, singing songs long forgotten; spies had crept past them; they had given shelter to many lovers, in their last hour of parting. And in the end, still erect, still immaculate — these pillars, whose delicate classical exteriors sheltered hearts of British oak — had faced the final battle, the Battle of Britain.

At all costs, I had to have them.

'Are they very expensive, Mr. Crowther?'

'Eh?' He, too, had been dreaming. He blinked himself back to reality. 'Expensive . . . the pillars?' He chuckled. 'I wouldn't worry about that, Mr. Beverley. Eight, did you say? Better have ten, to be on the safe side. One never knows, with a Folly. I'll have them sent along next week.'

To this day he has never sent me a bill.

So here is the picture we promised you. I do hope you like it. It was rather difficult for Willie to get everything in, as we were not equipped with a helicopter, but you can see the balustrade, with the steps, and the edge of the pool, and the peculiar crane with its morbid habits, and another flight of steps, and then the pillars. If you think that they appear pretentious, you must remember that the trees behind them are still comparatively young. In ten years they will be towering over the columns, and then it will all look much more natural and — I hope — faintly mysterious, so that any woman who sits in the middle of them will feel, if she has any sensibility, like something by Fragonard.

However, though you can see the general scheme, there are a number of delectable details too small for illustration, and these I would like to describe.

First, the shrapnel scars. There proved to be three main scars in all, when the columns were finally set in place. I had such a special feeling about those scars, such a sense of pride and affection, that at the foot of one column I have planted a white rose, at the foot of another a white wisteria, and at the foot of the third an ivy with pale green leaves and white edges. They have grown slowly but surely, and are gently covering the scars, so that now, if you wish to see them, you must draw aside a little mantle of green leaves and white flowers.

White and silver has been the keynote of all the flowers and leaves that have been introduced into the stonework under the pillars. Along the path that leads to them is a border of lavender, and in the pockets are various centaureas, notably *dealbata* and *ragusina*, which look as though they are rimmed with frost even on the hottest days of summer. There are silver sages too, and the old-fashioned *stachys lanata*, which flops its rabbity ears all over the stone, and a miniature silver juniper, and in between the columns there are . . . but no, that would be a lie. In between the columns there are *not* great clusters of madonna lilies. There should be, but for some unaccountable reason they did not — to use a phrase of Oldfield's — 'coom oop'. Perhaps this was partly due to the fact that Four, Five and Seven played too conspicuous a role in their planting.

You cannot imagine how agreeable it is to sit beneath those columns, on a summer evening, looking out over one's small domain, with the white roses climbing over the balustrades, and the white lilies on the pool, and the shadow of the peculiar crane lengthening across the water . . . and then the steps, and the lawn, and the circular bed with the cupid perched over a mass of white stocks. And at the end of the garden the old brick wall, with the lane beyond it, and the fields in the distance, with the giant poplars standing like sentinels on the horizon.

Nor is it only on a summer evening that it is pleasant. For once, when visiting Mr. Crowther, I found a pair of eighteenth-century braziers, and sometimes, on frosty winter afternoons, we take out the braziers and pack them with kindling and coke and a top layer of fir-cones, and light them, and leave them to make a magic circle of warmth. Then, after dinner, we go out, wrapped up, with glasses of mulled claret in our hands, and we sit there enjoying the strangest physical sensations . . . tingling cold outside, glowing warmth within and all the great heavy curtains of the night about us, with silver sequins in their folds. And Four, Five and Seven join the party, sitting very close to the braziers and looking as if they were participating in some esoteric witches' conference. I have no doubt that this would not be everybody's cup of tea, and I suspect that it may end in double pneumonia or bankruptcy or both. But at least it is one way of relaxing, when the day's work is done, and it has inspired some pleasant and instructive interludes of conversation. To which, in the next chapter, we will refer.

CHAPTER XI

CONVERSATION PIECE

THE Folly, as you may have gathered from the previous pages, is now the centre of the garden and, *ipso facto*, the centre of my life, and it annoys me very much when my friends refer to it, irreverently, as Stonehenge. Admittedly, there are moments, round about eleven on a bleak February morning, when the casual observer might think that the Druids had been up to something at the bottom of the garden. But, then, the casual observer would not know about all the magic circumstances which had gone to its erection. He would not understand the romance of the shrapnel scars, nor would he appreciate the fact that — according to Willie McLaren — the whole design fitted into the mysterious geometry of Nature.

All these things would be explained to him at inordinate length, and by the time we had finished it is unlikely that the word Stonehenge would ever pass his lips again.

It was Our Rose who first christened the magic circle

Stonehenge — (she pronounced it Stoonhinge) — and this chapter is the result of that piece of impertinence. No woman should be allowed to say such things with impunity. Besides, it was this remark which led to the ensuing conversation piece, and that, in its turn, was the direct cause of the final flare-up between Rose and Miss Emily, with which we must later concern ourselves.

'Let us all go and sit in your sweet Stoonhinge,' said Rose, on this particular afternoon.

I can hear her saying it, in her cool, skimmed milk voice. I can see her saying it, too, in her cool, skimmed milk dress. It was a hot day, and she was dressed very suitably, in pale grey, with a wide picture hat of white straw and — of course — the moonstones. Miss Emily, on the other hand, was not so appropriately attired; she had just come from the funeral of a distant relative, and her melancholy garments hung heavily about her. There had been faint signs of a fracas from the moment they met. When Emily had commented upon her cool appearance, Rose had replied, with a tinkling laugh, that it was remarkable that she should look cool . . . considering.

'Considering what, dear?'

'Considering how hard I have been working on the herbaceous border.'

'In this heat? I should have thought you would have got sunstroke.'

'No, dear. I did not go outside. I treated it from my study. I did not work with my hands, but with my mind. However . . .' here she turned towards me, with a superior smile . . . 'we know how exhausting mental work can be, do we not?'

Miss Emily's mouth opened very wide, and there might have been an explosion at that very moment if Marius had not arrived.

During tea, Rose was just as irritating. The conversation, not unnaturally, turned towards the Folly, which was still something of a novelty. Marius, whose range of curious knowledge never fails to astonish me, launched into a dissertation on Follies and their history — the many weird grottoes, tombs, monuments and extravagances with which rich Englishmen have embellished their gardens in the past. Rose knew nothing whatever about the subject, but she pretended that she did, and whenever Marius referred to some obscure sanctuary or tower in a remote castle, she would nod wisely, and murmur, 'It has *always* fascinated me', or '*Quite* one of my favourites'. Or words to that effect.

In spite of her distracting commentary, Marius was able to tell us enough about these fascinating grotesques to make us wish to go on a tour of Britain in search of them. Who would suspect that in the setting of Skipton Castle there is a room built round a mother-of-pearl hermaphrodite? How many people have seen the sham castle in Bennington, with the statue of Buddha over the Norman archway? How often do tourists penetrate the thick woods at Rushton in search of the fabulous Triangular Lodge, built by Sir Thomas Tresham at the end of the sixteenth century? Sir Thomas was a mystic who was preoccupied by the numeral three, and in his grounds he erected an architectural triangle of the greatest complexity, in which every room and decoration expresses a variation on this number. Even the windows have three, six, or nine sides, and on the triangular roof nine gargoyles stare out into the dark glades through triple eyes.

'There is even a second Stonehenge,' said Marius, 'built in the eighteen-twenties on the Yorkshire moors by a local landowner. It is not, of course, as large as the original, but it is large enough, and — to me — it is strangely sinister.

For it has a Stone of Sacrifice, and I fancy that the Stone has been used.'

Rose gave an affected shudder. She rose to her feet. 'Too silly of us,' she said, 'sitting indoors on such a lovely afternoon, talking about such morbid things.' She walked to the window and looked out to the garden, where my Folly was gleaming in the sunlight. Then she clasped her hands and turned round to me.

'Stoonhinge!' she exclaimed.

I did not see the point.

'Your pillars!' She produced the silvery tinkle. 'Is that very naughty of me?'

I might have used a blunter adjective, but Miss Emily saved me from expressing an opinion. Rising from the sofa like a black figure of doom, she, too, went over to the window.

'I fail to see the connection,' she said, in the iciest of tones. 'However, it would be a charming setting for Marius to talk to us, if . . .' with a meaning glance at Rose . . . 'he is allowed to do so.'

'Yes. Do let us all go and sit in your sweet Stoonhinge!'

So without any more ado we went and sat in my sweet Stoonhinge.

II

It was *l'heure exquise.* A quarter to six on a warm summer evening. A cloudless sky, the scent of sunbaked grass, and a very faint breeze, just enough to rustle the bulrushes round the peculiar crane.

Here, surely, there should have been peace, and the perfect setting for elegant conversation. For a while, indeed, all was well. It was only when Miss Emily commented upon the remarkable growth of a clump of laurels that the first notes of discord began to be heard.

'Whenever I see a laurel,' said Marius, 'I shudder.'

This remark was regrettable, for Miss Emily was very proud of her laurel hedge. It was made even more regrettable by Our Rose, who nodded, and shuddered in sympathy, to show that she, too, was far too sensitive for so common a shrub as the laurel.

However, Rose had reacted rather too soon.

'I do not mean, of course, that I object to the laurel as such,' continued Marius, who was quite unaware of the silent conflict between the two ladies. 'In its wild state it is a noble creation of nature.' (Here Miss Emily shot a withering glance at Our Rose.) 'The reason I shudder is because I recall the terrible fate which might have been ours if we had lived in the classical age.' He turned to Rose. 'How would *you* like it, if you were picking flowers in a country lane, and suddenly found your feet turning to roots and your arms to branches?'

Rose, who had no idea what he was talking about, lowered her eyes and shook her head, to indicate that she would dislike it exceedingly.

'It was all Apollo's fault, of course,' continued Marius. 'It nearly always was Apollo's fault, don't you think?'

Rose, directly challenged, agreed that it was indeed.

'What was?' demanded Miss Emily. She was evidently determined to expose Rose's ignorance.

'Apollo, dear,' breathed Rose, with commendable vagueness.

'Quite. But why was it his fault? And what?'

'Well, dear. . . .'

Marius came to her rescue. 'What Rose meant, I imagine, was that if Apollo had not fallen in love with Daphne, and pursued her with such ardour, she would not have invoked the aid of her father Peneus, the river god, who in turn would not have been obliged to change her into a laurel.' He sighed and looked towards the coppice, where the laurels gleamed darkly in the fading light. 'Poor Daphne! I wonder if she is happy. Of course, Apollo did his best to make amends; he made her the symbol of every sort of glory. . . .'

He was interrupted by Rose, who was now fully *au courant* with the laurel situation. She turned to Miss Emily. 'Laurel wreaths, my dear. You see the connection?'

'I knew that a laurel wreath was a symbol of victory, if that is what you mean,' retorted Miss Emily. 'That is the sort of thing we *both* learned at school. But I was not familiar with the legend of Daphne.' The gimlet glance with which she accompanied this confession indicated that she was quite certain that Rose was not familiar with it either.

Marius was still unconscious of the heat that his remarks were engendering. 'Whenever one walks in a garden,' he resumed, 'one walks among the spirits of these unfortunate creatures who have been victims of the whims of the gods. What could have been more undeserved than the fate of poor Belides?'

He addressed his remark to Rose, who gave him a melancholy smile, that might have meant anything at all.

Miss Emily kept her eyes firmly on Rose. 'What happened to him?'

'Not him,' interrupted Marius. 'Her. Poor Belides was a nymph.' (Rose allowed herself to cast a pitying glance in Miss Emily's direction.) 'She had the ill-fortune to attract the attention of Vertumnus, who was, of course . . .' here he made a gesture of apology to Rose, 'the god of orchards.'

Rose nodded to Miss Emily. 'Orchards, dear,' she repeated.

Miss Emily looked as though she would explode. 'Yes,

dear. I heard him, too. And what happened then?'

'When she tried to escape, he turned her into a daisy, which is why the common daisy is called Bellis. It was, I think, very inconsiderate of him. Merely, because one is attractive, to be subjected to an infinity of lawn-mowers.'

He took up the idea, and played with it, and I wish that I might have taken notes of his talk, so light and airy and yet so informed with curious fragments of knowledge. I watched the shadows creeping across the lawn, and the little white ghosts of poor Belides gleaming on the grass. They were closing for the night, and they looked so frail and defenceless that I was in half a mind to tell Gaskin not to cut the lawn tomorrow . . . not, perhaps, to cut it ever again. The lawn should become a sanctuary to Belides.

As the eye of Marius roved round the garden, so these delicate memories were evoked. A cool breeze was stirring the branches of the almond trees behind us, and in their music he heard again the legend of Demophoon and Phyllis. So vividly did he recall the story that we seemed to be standing with her, waiting on the shores of Thrace, staring out to the empty seas which should have borne her lover back from Athens. Nine times she made her way to the shore, and at last, despairing, sank down and died. Then and there, in the dusk, an almond tree sprang up holding her spirit in its branches. And when, three months later, Demophoon returned, the tree broke into a spray of blossom, as a token of her forgiveness.

He spoke of Paralisos, too, the beautiful lad who died of grief for the loss of Melicerta, and was changed into a primrose. 'And perhaps it was for this reason,' he suggested, 'that Shakespeare made the primrose the funeral flower of youth. You remember those lines in *Cymbeline*?'

Rose gave a curious sort of twitch to her neck, which

might have meant 'yes' and might have meant 'no'. After which, she repeated the word *'Cymbeline'*, in a faint whisper, and stared straight ahead of her, firmly avoiding the eye of Miss Emily who was growing more and more sickened by these deceits.

Marius spoke the lines gently and quietly, allowing them to sing their own music. . . .

'With fairest flowers
Whilst summer last, and I live here, Fidele,
I'll sweeten thy sad grave; thou shalt not lack
The flower that's like thy face, pale Primrose.'

Rose sighed deeply, and turned to Miss Emily. 'Such beautiful lines, I always think.'

'Yes, dear. I'm sure you do. But how did Shakespeare propose to pick primroses in summer?'

Rose gave a patronizing smile. 'That is just a poetical conceit, dear.'

'Not at all. It is a botanical impossibility. Primroses finish in April and summer doesn't begin till June.'

'But these lines, dear, are eternal.' Rose's voice sounded curiously parsonic.

'If ever I heard a non-sequitur, that is one.'

I thought it time to pour oil on the troubled waters. 'The only legend I can remember,' I said, 'is the one about the bulrushes.'

Rose nodded in a superior way. 'Moses, of course.'

I was happy to be able to contradict her, thereby mollifying, for the moment, Miss Emily. 'I wasn't thinking of Moses, I was thinking of Midas.'

'Ah!'

Miss Emily leant forward. 'Surely, dear, *you* have heard of King Midas and the bulrushes?'

'To be quite frank, dear,' admitted Rose, with enormous condescension, 'I had not.'

'There must be a gap in your Encyclopaedia.'

This was terrible. I hurried into the story of Midas and the bulrushes, which was short and sweet. It was really a quarrel between two rival prima donnas, and once again — as Marius had observed — it was Apollo's fault. Apollo had sung to King Midas. So had Marsyas, the satyr. And Midas had been so tactless as to prefer the singing of Marsyas. Without any further ado, the outraged god clapped a pair of ass's ears on to him, and departed to Olympia in a fine thunder of indignation.

But that was not the end of the story. For the King's barber saw the ears, and, though he was sworn to secrecy, he whispered the terrible truth to the bulrushes that grew in the lake of the palace garden. And for ever afterwards, when the wind blows from the West, all the bulrushes that stand and dream by all the lakes all over the world are woken, and they bend and rustle and chuckle to one another . . . 'King Midas has ass's ears . . . King Midas has ass's ears!'

'In the case of Midas,' observed Marius, 'one can at least suggest that there was some justification for his punishment. But when one thinks of poor Philemon and Baucis. . . .'

Rose bowed her head in melancholy assent. Thoughts of Philemon and Baucis, she wished it to be understood, had often troubled her.

'Who *were* Philemon and Baucis?' demanded Miss Emily, addressing her remarks directly to Our Rose.

Rose, with a weary smile, inclined her neck towards Marius. 'He can tell you, dear, so much better than I can.'

'I have no doubt about that,' snorted Miss Emily. 'But I was asking *you*.'

For the first time it must have occurred to Marius that Our Rose's knowledge of the classics was perhaps less extensive than he had imagined. And since he was a kindly person, who would have hated to think that his own erudition should be the cause of distress to others, he deftly extricated Rose from her embarrassment.

'You flatter me,' he said to Miss Emily, 'when you suggest that I know more about these things than others. I only remember the main outlines.' He turned to Rose. 'Correct me if I am wrong. We begin with Jupiter and Mercury — descending in human form from Olympus. Agreed?'

Rose inclined her head.

'The scene moves to the plains of Phrygia. . . .'

Miss Emily interrupted him. 'Where did he say, dear?'

'Fridgier,' repeated Rose, without a moment's hesitation.

Miss Emily drew in a sharp breath, with the obvious intention of saying something quite devastating, but Marius was too quick for her.

'And there,' he continued, at heightened speed, 'the drama began. They called at house after house, but were always turned away, till they came to the aged Philemon, who lived with his wife Baucis, in poverty. . . .'

'The *direst* poverty,' prompted Rose, who felt that here she was on a safe wicket. Miss Emily merely glared at her in contempt.

'The direst poverty,' agreed Marius, graciously. 'In spite of this, they entertained the gods with fruit and wine. Afterwards, they walked with them to the top of a neighbouring hill. . . .'

'And then?' Miss Emily had leant so close to Rose that I feared she would bite her.

'*He* will tell you, dear,' said Rose. 'Such a very beautiful legend.'

It was too much for Miss Emily. She gave up the vain attempt to expose Rose's ignorance, and Marius finished his story in peace. I shall not pretend, like Rose, that it was familiar to me. Nor do I agree, with Rose, that it was 'very beautiful'. It seemed to me rather unkind.

Jupiter and Mercury, it seems, were so angry with the people who had not asked them to dine that they sent down a roaring torrent to destroy them. That was bad enough. But their method of thanking Philemon and Baucis was even worse. One day, when Philemon was offering sacrifices to the gods, he saw Baucis walking up the steps towards him — turning into a lime tree.

Let Marius finish the story. 'Not unnaturally, Philemon commented upon this phenomenon, which is uncommon, even in the most advanced circles. No sooner had he spoken than he saw the faces of Jupiter and Mercury in the heavens, and discovered similar symptoms in himself. His arms were sprouting, roots were pushing from the soles of his feet, and there was a green film over his eyes. Soon, both he and his wife were lime trees from top to toe, and so they remained for several hundred years, until they died. I often wonder if, from time to time, they had not a strong desire to sit down.'

I had sometimes been disturbed by the same fancy myself, indeed, I once wrote a fairy tale about it.[1] There are three old poplars in the field opposite my study which, I am quite certain, are longing to sit down, if only they could manage it. However, it was growing too late to indulge these fancies, and so I led the way back to the house, taking Miss Emily firmly by the arm, and keeping her as far as possible from Our Rose.

[1] *The Tree that Sat Down.* Cape.

CHAPTER XII

OVER THE FENCE

UNTIL the final battle between Our Rose and Miss Emily, which it is now my sad duty to relate, there had been so little discord in Meadowstream that sometimes I had thought it must be an enchanted place, with a special virtue in the air that blows in from the hills.

The only storms that had ruffled our society had been storms in the most delicate teacups . . . though perhaps that is an unsuitable metaphor. You could not put Mrs. Maples's cow, for example, in a teacup, and Mrs. Maples's cow had been one of the rare instigators of a neighbourly dispute.

Mrs. Maples is the very charming lady who lives in the rambling old house at the end of the lane — the house with the faded blue shutters and the big field with the poplars and the pines, which forms the foreground of most of my life. That field is usually a peaceful rural canvas, dotted from time to time with agreeable and . . . to a writer . . . undistracting natural phenomena. True, there are some-times geese, which set up a great cackle, but for some reason or other I do not object to them. They make me think of the chorus of an opera by Mr. Alan Rawsthorne. And there are ponies, which make charmingly hysterical sounds as they scamper about in spring. And rooks, of course, whose music is to me of the greatest beauty — a wild, melancholy chant, which would surely have gone to the heart of Emily Brontë.

All these notes in the Meadowstream symphony were harmonious, or capable of being transmuted into harmony. It was only the cow that jarred. For it was one of those cows that insist, from time to time, upon having calves, and whenever its calf was taken away, it appeared to regard me as personally responsible, and spent its entire day glaring at me through a gap in the hedge, emitting foghorn noises which impeded — to say the least of it — the smooth marshalling of such thoughts as I was trying to give to the world.

This led to an interchange of notes. Not angry notes, but notes in which there was a definite divergence of opinion. On my side there was an appeal to art. How could one write sparkling dialogue to the accompaniment of sounds which recalled a film of the sinking of the *Titanic*, drifting to its doom with the foghorn wailing to the attendant Fates? On Mrs. Maples's side there was an appeal to Nature, and to reason. Calves, it seemed, had to be taken away, and cows, not unnaturally, resented it. But cows had short memories, and if I would only endure the foghorn for a few days longer, it would eventually die down to an occasional murmur. Which, of course, it did.

The only other trouble has arisen from cockerels. Perhaps I am unduly sensitive about cockerels because once, in London, I had to seek police protection from them. I was living in a small house in Hampstead, and one day the lady next door, in a sentimental mood, bought twelve little fluffy darlings which she fondly imagined were pullets. They grew, with surprising speed, into gigantic, scarlet-faced monsters with throats of brass. They swaggered round her garden, looking as if they had just stepped off a space-ship. And they began their frightening, strangled shrieks long before dawn.

I wrote to the lady, pointing out that my residence was also my place of business — and business was suffering. At the time I was composing the score of a revue for the Saville Theatre, most of it in the key of D Flat Major, and the cockerels' screams were tuned to the key of F Sharp Minor. This, she must agree, would lead to confusion; I did not want the leading lady to be mistaken for a cockerel. My neighbour did not agree; she did not even answer. So I found her number in the telephone book, and one day, in the small hours of the morning, I rang her up. After a time I heard a sleepy voice inquiring: 'Who is it? What is the matter?' I replied with a volley of cockerel noises, which I had been practising for some time. They were startlingly realistic, and they were delivered with real passion. Then I rang off.

These hostilities continued for about a week. However, I could not go on sitting up half the night making cockerel noises, so eventually I went to the police, and they gave me a form called 'Noisy Animals' — or something like that. And that settled the lady's hash, and the cockerels were taken away in a van, and I stood at the window and waved to them, which greatly enraged the lady. Then I went back to the piano and wrote a beautiful serenade in D Flat Major . . . with just one modulation into F Sharp Minor, to show that there was no ill-feeling.

How we do run on. All I really intended to say was that even the cockerels, in Meadowstream, seem slightly muted, and comparatively concordant. Once, in a nearby cottage, there was a bantam with a very shrewish disposition, but I bought it — at an excessive price — and packed it off to

Scotland. For the rest, the cockerels sound but faintly, and their curious sharps and trebles blend into the broad symphony of Nature, contributing a tone that is astringent but not entirely displeasing.

It was because of this long reign of peace in Meadowstream, this absence of any neighbourly hostilities, that the sudden outbreak of war between Miss Emily and Our Rose made so startling an impact on our lives.

II

True, there had been menacing signs and portents, as we saw in the last chapter. And as the days went by, it was only too evident that Miss Emily was nearing explosion point. The root cause of the trouble lay in Rose's extravagant claims to be a floral spirit-healer.

'I've always admitted that there may be something in it for human beings,' Miss Emily snorted to me one day. 'In fact, I believe there *is*. Anyway, it can't do any harm if a few Harley Street specialists are made to sit up and take notice. But plants . . . no. Do you know her latest? Greenfly!'

'You don't mean to say. . .?'

'I *do* mean to say. She says that people who have greenfly on their roses are mental; no, that's not quite right, it's the greenfly that is mental . . . or some such nonsense. She told me that *she* never sprays her roses, she just thinks about them.'

'Whatever did you say to that?'

A gleam came into Miss Emily's eye. 'I'm afraid I was rather rude. I asked her if she breathed on them as well.'

'Oh dear!'

'Well . . . it was a perfectly legitimate question. Those

violet cachous she's always sucking would be enough to put paid to a Colorado beetle.'

Things, I feared, were coming to a pretty pass.

But it was the dispute over the weeds in Rose's orchard that finally brought matters to a head.

I was made aware of this trouble on a summer afternoon of such golden beauty that it would have seemed impossible for any note of discord to intrude. I had called on Miss Emily to return to her a book which she had lent me on fuchsias. (I was going through a period of acute fuchsia intoxication — and indeed I still am. Fuchsias are among my ninety-nine most favourite flowers — like Elsa Maxwell's ninety-nine most intimate friends. I could go on for hours, and probably shall, one day, about their white petticoats and their crimson ruffs and the incredible grace with which they dispose themselves.)

Emily was having tea in the garden, and asked me to join her. We had China tea, which I greatly dislike, but it did not matter, because the sun was hot and caressing, and the shadows under the lime trees were purple and thickly painted, and summer was at her most sensuous hour. Even Emily, in spite of the military cut of her hair and the steely glint that never quite left her eyes, had a feminine allure. She had a fine profile, a lissom figure, beautiful hands . . . it was strange that she had never married.

Or was it? Perhaps that question was answered by the drama that was about to begin.

III

Suddenly Emily thrust out her hands, and clapped them sharply together.

'There's another!' she cried.

I imagined that she had caught a mosquito. 'Some people say that lavender keeps them off.'

'I was not catching insects.' She opened her palm, disclosing a seed of thistledown. 'A little present from dear Rose!'

'Why from Rose?'

'Her orchard is a mass of weeds — a positive jungle. Nestles and thittles — I mean nettles and thistles — as high as your shoulder. Docks like small trees. Whenever the wind is in the right direction they come floating over by the million. What my herbaceous border will be like next year I dread to think.'

'Couldn't you ask her to cut them down?'

'I've asked her a dozen times. No. Perhaps not a dozen. But at least four. And I've written her two letters.'

'What did she say?'

'She didn't even answer the letters. And whenever I've mentioned the subject she's gone off into a lot of nonsense about wild flowers and hating to cut them down. Considering she makes a large income by sawing off the heads of daffodils and forcing them into inverted pin-cushions it seems peculiar that she should be so sensitive.'

She thrust out her hand again, and caught another seed of thistledown.

'The whole air's thick with them,' she complained. I looked around, and could see nothing. 'At least, it would be if the wind were my way. As it is, it's blowing over to her.'

Suddenly a gleam came into her eyes. 'That reminds me. My rubbish heap. I'm quite sure there are a lot of weeds on it, and they might drift into Rose's garden. I really think I ought to light it.'

'I hardly think . . .' I began.

'Oh, but if the weeds did blow over, Rose would be **quite**

Evening

justified in complaining. I should hate to give her the chance of saying that I didn't practice what I preached.'

She had already risen to her feet. 'Shall we go? I know how you love making bonfires.'

I followed with some reluctance. It is true that I love a good bonfire, on a December afternoon, when the heart of the fire is like a red jewel, and in the growing darkness the white smoke plumes upwards like the feathers of some fabulous bird. Bonfires, then, are among the rarest joys of man's existence. But not on a torrid afternoon of August, in one's best Sunday suit.

The rubbish heap was at the bottom of Emily's kitchen garden, and was separated from Rose's property by only a short hedge of laurels. It proved to be more substantial than I had expected. Indeed, it was difficult to understand how Emily had accumulated such a large collection of decaying vegetable matter at this time of the year, to say nothing of rotting sacks, worn out strips of linoleum, potato peelings, and what looked like the contents of several dustbins. Moreover, there were signs that it had been only recently in a state of eruption, for the grass all around was singed for a space of several yards.

The breeze was beginning to freshen. 'You don't think it would be better to wait?' I suggested.

'Certainly not. This wind will soon be blowing things all over the place.'

It would need a very strong wind, I reflected, to lift so many damp cabbage stalks and such large strips of decayed linoleum. However, I obediently lit the fire in the place where Emily directed, where there was a bundle of suspiciously fresh kindling, and in a few moments it was blazing away in a mixture of hot flame and thick, greasy smoke, that streamed towards the laurel hedge.

'Beautiful!' cried Miss Emily. 'Quite beautiful! How right you were, when you wrote that chapter about the fun of making fires!'

I could not recall having written any such chapter, but I did not argue about it. I was too apprehensive. The object of the bonfire was obvious; it was a form of counter-attack in the larger Battle of the Weeds. I could only hope that Rose was out for the afternoon.

We wandered back to the tea-table. It would have looked cowardly if I had beat an immediate retreat. Besides, Emily would have been offended if I had not finished my piece of walnut layer cake. Apart from that — if we are being frank — I was beginning to feel a sort of awful fascination, wondering what was going to happen.

We had not long to wait. After some five minutes' desultory conversation, during which our eyes constantly strayed towards the Vesuvius-like mounds of smoke that were darkening the sky, the wicket gate swung open and Rose came hurrying up the path.

She was hatless and her hair was untidy; the moonstone necklace was hanging askew; and she was breathing very quickly, as though she had been running a race. I also noticed that there was a smut on the end of her nose.

She sketched me a brief smile, and addressed herself immediately to Emily.

'Dear Emily . . . such a silly little matter . . . but your bonfire, dear.'

'What about it?'

'Billowing into my garden. We shall all be quite kippered.'

As she spoke, the wind — as it sometimes does in summer — made a roundabout turn, and drifts of smoke began to swirl in our direction. Emily seized upon this happy chance.

'Really, dear,' she said, 'I fancied that the wind was blowing *my* way.'

Rose did not seem to hear her. She was emitting a rapid succession of dramatic coughs, that recalled the guttural noises made by the Mimis of amateur operatic companies.

'Forgive me,' she murmured. 'My throat.' Quite a thick wave of smoke engulfed us for a moment. I awaited another succession of coughs. But Rose had made her point. 'Better!' she breathed, and forced a smile . . . only to change it, a moment later, to an expression of deep disgust.

She took a step forward towards the lavender bed. 'May I?' she murmured, bending down to pick a couple of sprays. She crushed them in the palm of her hand, and pressed them to her face, closing her eyes in symbolic gratitude, inhaling the perfume as though it were sent as a sort of heavenly deliverance.

'Such a relief!' She turned to Emily. 'What *is* it, dear, that you are burning?'

Even as she spoke, the wind changed back to its prevailing direction; Vesuvius resumed its assault on Rose's domains, and we were left — atmospherically — in peace.

'What is it, dear?' she repeated.

'What is what?'

'What are you burning on your rubbish heap?'

Emily raised her eyebrows. 'What does one usually burn on rubbish heaps?'

'I really don't know, dear. Judging from the present variety I would suppose that it was dead cows . . . yes? Or some extraordinarily poisonous chemical? Or perhaps one's oldest hats?' This last suggestion was a very telling thrust, for Emily's favourite economy was her hats. She frequently appeared in hats which looked as if they had long been discarded from the collection of the late Queen Mary.

Emily bared her teeth. 'Rose is so amusing,' she hissed.

Rose also bared her teeth. 'Which is not always so easy, dear, when one is being asphyxiated.'

'Really, Rose, do kindly keep a sense of proportion. You speak as if the end of the world had come, merely because I burn a few weeds.'

Weeds! The fatal word had been spoken.

Rose closed her eyes and shook her head. 'Weeds!' she repeated, with a sigh of weariness. 'Please do not let us talk about weeds!'

'I quite understand you don't wish to talk about them. . . .'

'There are pleasanter subjects of conversation.'

'There are also pleasanter objects to come drifting into one's garden by the ton.'

Rose gave her tinkling laugh. 'My dear, I think it is for you to keep a sense of proportion. No weeds ever had such a hideous aroma as you have been creating.'

'That is not the point.'

'No? I thought it was precisely the point. If I am to be choked to death by your smoke. . . .'

'And if my garden is to be choked out of existence by your weeds. . . .'

There was an awful pause. One could almost hear the gauntlets being thrown on to the crazy paving. The battle had begun. But by some curious feminine quirk, both ladies chose to fight it — as it were — obliquely; each became, of a sudden, unaware of the other's existence, and addressed her remarks directly to me. I tried to assume an expression of amiable impartiality, turning my head from side to side, making non-committal grunts. It was highly embarrassing, for they kept edging nearer and nearer to me, to emphasize each point, until our faces were nearly touching. The dialogue went something like this:

199

ROSE   I'm afraid that dear Emily does not seem to share our love of flowers.

EMILY   If she is referring to forests of thistles and nettles and docks. . . .

ROSE   (*Ignoring her.*) They seem to love growing in my little orchard. . . .

EMILY   The thistles and nettles, yes. (That was what she intended to say, but she was so agitated that in fact she said 'thestles and nittles', which drew from Rose a frosty smile.)

ROSE   (*In fluting tones.*) Foxgloves, evening primroses, meadowsweet . . . such beautiful names, I always think.

EMILY   There's nothing very beautiful about . . . (here she paused to make sure of getting it right) . . . thistles and nettles and docks.

ROSE   I could not bear to cut the wild flowers down. Apart from that, as Emily knows very well, I need them for my work. My rustic arrangements, you know.

EMILY   If she would make some rustic arrangements about the . . . (*pause*) . . . thistles and nettles and docks. . . .

ROSE   (*Turning sharply on her for a moment.*) Really, Emily . . . you are really developing an obsession, with your . . . (*pause*) . . . thistles and nettles and docks.

I was beginning to feel quite dizzy. At any moment, I felt, one of the ladies would trip up into nottles and thestles and dicks, and then where should we be?

EMILY   (*Directly to me, with a grating cackle of laughter.*) I think we might have something to say about obsessions, when we think of the excitement caused by our little bonfire.

ROSE   (*Smiling fiercely.*) Some people would call it a holocaust. . . .

EMILY   I have been making fires in this garden for twenty years. . . .

ROSE   Really! It is a wonder that there is any green vegetation left in the neighbourhood.

EMILY   Twenty years. And during all that period nobody else has complained of my smoke!

ROSE   (*With a sudden flash of inspiration.*) I have been growing wild flowers in my orchard for fifteen years. And during all that period nobody else has complained of my weeds!

Both ladies by now were shouting; both ladies were standing very erect, with their chins held high. It was one of the most painful moments in the whole history of Meadowstream. The conflict seemed all the sharper because of the idyllic background against which it was set. Blue skies and yellow sunshine on green grass — the scent of lavender and the hum of bees — lazy purple shadows under the limes. The only dark feature in this pastoral scene was the grey octopus of smoke that continued to weave its loathsome limbs over the laurel hedge and occasionally . . . for the wind was still fickle . . . stretching a peppery tentacle in our direction.

It was one of those changes of wind that, mercifully, broke the tension. A thick arm of smoke swept right across us, completely concealing us from each other for a space of several seconds. When it cleared away again, the ladies had abandoned their heroic positions, and their eyes were watering so painfully that they were no longer in a condition to transfix one another with glassy stares.

I seized the opportunity. In a moment of inspiration I said: 'Supposing we toss for it?'

The ladies transferred their glares — or rather, their blinks — to me. I wished that I had not spoken, but it was too late to draw back. I drew a coin from my pocket. I turned to Emily.

'Heads, the weeds are cut down.'

Rose made an impatient gesture. 'I still maintain that the word "weeds". . . .'

I was not going to let her interrupt. 'Rose, my dear, please let me finish.'

Miss Emily nodded. 'He is quite right. Let us see what he has to suggest.' Even as she spoke I realized that my idea had been a happy one. Miss Emily was an inveterate gambler.

'Heads,' I repeated — and for courtesy's sake I changed the phrase — 'Rose scythes her orchard.'

'Thank you,' breathed Rose.

'In which case you . . .' turning to Emily . . . 'find another place for your bonfire.'

'I really do not see . . .' Then she closed her lips. 'Very well.'

'And if it is tails?' Rose had put on her cooing voice, and was all gentility. She pronounced it 'teels'. This was a danger sign. 'And if it is teels?' When Rose became genteel it was a sure proof that savage emotions were stirring in her breast.

I hurried on. 'If it is teels — tails, you do not cut down your . . . I mean, you don't have to scythe the orchard, and Emily does not have to move her bonfire.'

'So that I shall be perpetually kippered with smoke?'

Miss Emily chimed in. 'And I shall be perpetually smothered in thestles . . . thistles . . . and all the rest of it?'

'You can't have it both ways.'

There was an awful silence.

It was suddenly broken by Rose, with the lightest of laughs. 'Really, Emily dear, we are not being very . . . how do you say? . . . *sporting?*' She pronounced this not very exotic word as if it were of foreign origin . . . almost as though it were spelt spoor . . . r . . . teeng. This was, of course, her intention. She wished to indicate that she, the artist, moved in a different world from the matter-of-fact Miss Emily. She, poor little Bohemian thing, did not really understand what was going on at all; she was bewildered by zese spoor . . . r . . . teeng peoples, is it not so? But like a true Bohemian, she was willing to trust all to the spin of a coin, for that . . . messieurs, mesdames, c'est la vie, n'est-ce pas? Hein?

If you think that I am reading too much into a mere intonation of a single word, it can only be because I have failed most lamentably to indicate the complexities of Rose's character. That phrase . . . 'how do you say . . . spoor . . . r . . . teeng?' was very sinister. It meant that she was feeling on top of the world, in command of the situation. It meant that, as far as she was concerned, the 'vibrations' were right.

And I swear that Rose, in this crucial moment, was 'vibrating' herself. From some deep alchemic reservoir of her spirit she was summoning up dark powers to guide that coin to the destiny she desired. It was really quite alarming. I fancied that I could feel my hand trembling to her bidding.

I span the coin. Very clumsily, because I am not good at spinning coins, nor — for that matter — throwing balls, nor tossing cabers, nor delivering straight lefts, nor doing any of those things which are so admired in the truly male. (It is conceivable that the reader may have detected signs of this degeneracy in previous passages.)

It made a clumsy circle and fell, with a mocking tinkle, under the garden seat. Both ladies made sudden darting movements, and then stopped in their tracks, as though frozen. Both ladies smiled. It was a tense, awful moment.

But Rose's vibrations won. When I bent down, and very slowly . . . to show there was no deception . . . held up the coin, teels were triumphant. The Queen's head was underneath. I remember thinking that this was strangely symbolic. The Hon. Emily Kaye, queen of Meadowstream, was biting the dust.

CHAPTER XIII

BATTLE

O N the following day the heavens blackened, and for several hours a violent thunderstorm raged over Meadowstream — a real old-fashioned pantomime thunderstorm, with titans standing in the wings, dropping bricks on to sheets of steel, and the sky's dark backcloth lit with the flickering, electric tails of demons.

I stood at the window, watching this atmospheric melodrama with mixed feelings. We wanted the rain, but storms always terrified the cats, especially Five, who for the next forty-eight hours would be confined to the linen-cupboard. I was not sure about Seven, either; it was his first storm, and every time there was a clap of thunder he arched his back and spat. One could only trust that this would not lead to any delayed psychological disturbances. Apart from the cats there were the auratum lilies, whose delicate petals were not carved to withstand such assaults. I dreaded to think how they would look when it was over.

On the whole, however, I was glad of the storm, because of the damping effect that it might have on the feud between Emily and Our Rose. It would certainly extinguish Emily's bonfire, and it could hardly fail to batter down a considerable quantity of Rose's weeds. Even nittles and . . .

nettles and thistles and docks . . . must be discouraged by such a deluge.

My hopes were short-lived. By six o'clock the skies had cleared again; the heavens were azure and immaculate; and a hot wind sprang up from the south-east, drying the lawns and parching the flower-beds. I made a rapid calculation. A south-east wind would blow directly from Rose's property into Emily's garden; it would give new life to the nettles, etc.; and though it would enable Emily's bonfire to be re-established as a weapon of attack, it would also negative its offensive value because it would blow all the smoke into her own face.

It was all deeply disturbing. One could only hope that the wind would die down, or that some sort of peculiar pest would afflict the thistles and the docks — or, best of all, that one or other of the ladies would decide to beat a retreat.

None of these hopes was realized. The wind blew on; no miraculous plague of locusts descended from the heavens, and the two ladies, on the few occasions when they came face to face, were afflicted with a total blindness to each other's presence.

The conflict, very evidently, was still far from its conclusion.

II

About a week later the wind at last subsided, to everybody's great relief. It had been getting on our nerves; a sirocco is bad enough in the South of France; in an English village it is insupportable. At last it would be possible to go out and stake the zinnias and prop up the stocks without fearing that they would be all blown down again by the morning. I looked forward to a few peaceful, productive days. In this spirit, one afternoon, I filled my pockets with bass, equipped myself with a bundle of bamboos, and walked across the lawn for a blissful afternoon in the herbaceous border.

But it was not to be. Just as I was about to begin, a familiar figure appeared at the bend in the lane, and strode rapidly towards me.

It was Our Rose, dressed in her heather-mixture tweed, with the garnets to match, and as soon as I saw these fatal jewels, I knew that there was thunder in the air. Rose, being exceptionally sensitive to 'vibrations', was inclined to match her costume to her mood. Her normal mood was serenity — (it would be unkind to describe it as self-satis-faction) — and this was expressed by silvery taffetas, dim blue silks, and, of course, the moonstone necklace. It was only when she was disturbed, and when — as she was the first to confess — her 'aura' was 'muddy' — that she felt obliged to clothe herself in the heather mixture, and give outward expression to the mental disturbance by means of the garnets. I once inquired of her whether, in such states of agitation, it would not be wiser to wear the moonstones, which might exert a soothing influence by bathing her spirit in the cool beams of their radiance. I was gently snubbed, and told that I did not understand these things. There would be a 'clash', it seemed, between the moon-stones and the agitation, and the last state would be worse than the first. If there was one thing that Rose could not abide, it was a 'clash'. It upset the vibrations.

It was useless to pretend that I was not at home, so I went out to greet her, and we walked over to the water-garden. I hoped that its gentle ripples, and the shadows of the rushes, might calm her down. But no. As soon as she was seated she turned to me and said: 'It is *so* good of you to give me your time. I greatly need your advice.' She fingered the garnets. 'A literary matter.'

For a moment I felt relieved. If it was only a question of literature. . . .

'It concerns a letter,' she went on. 'A letter which I have written to dear Emily. I should so like to read it to you, to see if you approve.'

My feeling of relief vanished as quickly as it had come. The very last thing I desired was to become involved in a dispute between Our Rose and Miss Emily.

Rose must have noticed my expression of dismay, for she hurried on before I could say anything. 'There is nothing in the least confidential in it. *I* have nothing to hide . . . nothing! Of course, if Emily wishes to surround her entire garden with a fence a hundred feet high, that is her affair. *Why* she should wish to do so, one has no idea; there may be reasons . . . she may have something that she wishes to conceal from the world . . . it might even be her herbaceous border, which is certainly nothing to be proud of. However, that is no concern of *mine*. My one desire is to be *neighbourly*. Anything else. . . .'

She finished the sentence with a wave of her hand. This gesture was evidently intended to indicate airy disdain; to me it suggested a tigress clawing at an imaginary victim.

'I don't quite understand . . .' I began.

'How foolish of me! How *could* you understand? Indeed, how can *anybody* understand? Sometimes one really wonders whether poor Emily is quite . . .' She tapped her forehead. 'It concerns my fence. Or rather, Emily's fence. The fence between my property and Emily's little garden.'

'I didn't know there was any.'

'My dear — I *knew* you would hit the nail on the head!' She made a grateful peck at my hand. 'That's the whole point. *Nobody* knew there was a fence — or that there should be a fence — or rather that Emily *thinks* there should be a fence. . . .'

Her explanation was somewhat incoherent, so I will endeavour to give a precis of the situation, as it emerged from a torrent of words, gestures, pecks, pauses and ironic laughs.

It appeared that there was, indeed, the broken-down remains of a fence between the properties of the two ladies. It ran for a distance of about a hundred yards, bounded on one side by Rose's orchard and on the other by a shrubbery that backed on to Miss Emily's kitchen garden. It was half way down a ditch, and consisted of a few lengths of decayed chestnut paling, one or two broken stumps, and some tangled strands of rusty wire. It seemed to serve no useful purpose, from Rose's account of it, and I believed that she was telling the truth when she assured me that she had no idea that there was a fence at all — until this happened.

'This' was a letter from Miss Emily, informing her that the fence was in a shocking state, that it was unsightly, and that it must be repaired, at Rose's expense, at the earliest possible opportunity. Miss Emily's 'advisers' had assured her that the fence was Rose's sole responsibility.

'Is it?' I asked. 'Is it your sole responsibility?'

She gave a scornful laugh. 'My dear, what has that got to do with it?'

'I should have thought it had quite a lot to do with it. If it is a matter of law. . . .'

'It is not a matter of law. It is a matter of principle.'

'The two are sometimes connected.'

'Not so often as one would wish. I don't care if I'm told to repair that fence by the Prime Minister and the Commander-in-Chief and the entire House of Lords. I will *not* do it. Why? Because there is not the faintest necessity for a fence. Until that business of the weeds. . . .'

'The weeds? Oh yes, I remember.'

'Until that little affair, in which Emily was made to look so very foolish, Emily never bothered about whether there was a fence there or not. Why should she? She's merely being tiresome — trying to get her own back — pretending to stand up for her rights. . . .'

'But if it *is* her right to have a fence there, legally. . . .'

'How can it possibly be her right, when it is so obviously wrong?'

I could think of no immediate reply to this question. There seemed no alternative but to listen to the letter, which Rose was impatient to read to me.

III

'*Miss Rose Fenton presents her compliments to the Hon. Emily Kaye.* . . .'

She paused. 'Do you think "Hon." is suitable? Or would you prefer "Honourable"?'

I was not very keen on either variation. I suggested that they both seemed rather formal.

'Oh but, my dear, we *must* be formal. Neighbourly, by all means, but formal, too. Then there will be no chance of misunderstandings. On the whole, I think "Hon." is better. It is more terse. It helps to set the mood. Polite but firm.'

She drew a deep breath. I realized that this was a literary composition over which she had expended considerable pains.

'. . . *the Hon. Emily Kaye,*' she resumed, '*and begs to inform her that she heartily reciprocates her desire to be neighbourly. Ever since Miss Fenton took up residence in*

Meadowstream, this has been her sole desire. And until the present dispute, she has been under the impression that this desire was reciprocated. Miss Fenton's property is perhaps somewhat more extensive than that of the Hon. Emily Kaye. . . .'

(Half an acre at the most, I thought, if she includes the gravel pit. But I let it pass.)

'. . . *and it is therefore possible that Miss Fenton has a wider experience in maintaining the boundaries of a country estate. This being so, she feels it her duty to inform the Hon. Emily Kaye that at no time has any of her neighbours requested — let alone demanded — the erection of any such edifice as the Hon. Emily Kaye now suggests.*'

I happened to glance over Rose's shoulder while she was reading this impressive passage. I could not help observing that the manuscript was tangled with corrections and re-corrections, with erasures and substitutions and insertions. It was increasingly obvious that Rose regarded this as her masterpiece.

She paused, and looked up for approval. 'Any criticisms?'

'I'm not quite sure about the word "edifice". It would seem to imply some sort of a building.'

'But that is precisely what she *does* imply.'

'Really? Has she said so?'

'Not in so many words. But surely it is obvious?'

It was not at all obvious to me, but Rose spoke so sharply, and tapped her foot so impatiently, that I had not the courage to contradict.

'If I admitted that I had to put up a fence at all, I should be finished. Emily would demand the most expensive fence one can buy. She might demand a brick wall . . . she probably *would* demand a brick wall. You see, my dear, I know the way her mind works. I am *devoted* to Emily, and always shall be, but I *do* understand her. May I continue? Thank you.'

She took another deep breath, and repeated the word 'edifice'. She went on:

'*In view of the fact that none of her other neighbours have suggested the desirability of a fence, Miss Fenton is puzzled by the Hon. Emily Kaye's sudden demand that one should be erected. She is also puzzled by the Hon. Emily Kaye's complaint that the existing fence — which consists of a few small rustic stakes, most of them in a recumbent position — is "unsightly". As this "fence" is surrounded, on both sides, by a thick belt of laurels, it is almost totally invisible from either of the properties. Indeed, Miss Fenton is informed by her advisers that the only point from which it can be espied at all is from the roof of the Hon. Emily Kaye's conservatory, and she finds it difficult to believe that the Hon. Emily Kaye can spend very much of her time in so elevated a position.*'

She looked up again. She was evidently thirsting for praise of the passage which she had just read.

'A little ironic, perhaps?' she suggested.

'Well . . .' I began.

'A shade *cruel*?' She was almost smacking her lips. 'Yes? I can see you think so. But isn't this one of those occasions when one must be cruel to be kind?'

'Are you quite sure that the only place from which the fence can be seen. . . .'

'Espied,' corrected Rose firmly. 'I think that was the word I used.'

'Espied . . . is the roof of the greenhouse?'

'Quite. When dear Emily was in London last week I set my alarm clock for five o'clock, and went into her garden to see for myself.'

This cast a somewhat different light on Rose's 'advisers'.

'In that case,' I admitted, 'it really does seem rather unnecessary. . . .'

'Unnecessary?' She produced her 'tinkling' laugh. (The tinkle was growing very shrill.) 'That is hardly the word! Unnecessary! It is totally and absolutely monstrous. It is the most blatant persecution, and I intend to fight it, whatever the cost. If Emily wishes to spend the rest of her life balancing on the top of her greenhouse, merely in order to annoy me, that is her affair. I shall not even notice it. If I should find myself in the vicinity, I should look the other way. And I should be extremely sorry if she fell off and broke her neck. *Extremely.*'

Her flashing eyes and heaving bosom, on which the garnets seemed to burn with a fiercer fire, somewhat detracted from the conviction of this statement.

She forced a smile and turned back to the manuscript. 'Only a few more words,' she said, 'but I think they are to the point.'

'Miss Fenton is equally puzzled by the Hon. Emily Kaye's complaint that the fence, in its present condition, "serves no utilitarian purpose". She would be grateful if the Hon. Emily Kaye would inform her what "purpose" she has in mind. The only possible "purpose" of a fence which occurs to Miss Fenton would be to prevent the passage of dangerous or destructive animals. Of course, it may be that the Hon. Emily Kaye intends, in the near future, to cultivate hyena or wild boar. In which case. . . .'

She paused with a smile of satisfaction. 'I felt that a little sarcasm was permissible. I do hope dear Emily will appreciate it.' Then she paused, as if in doubt. 'Should I perhaps have put the animals in the plural? Hyenas? Wild boars?'

'Are they necessary at all?'

'Oh — I think so. They give a lighter touch. Which

would you advise? Hyena — hyenas? I think I prefer the singular.'

I should have preferred neither. However, Rose was so evidently attached to these creatures of her imagination that I had not the heart to eliminate them. I agreed that the singular was more effective.

She nodded. 'Quite. I thought you would feel so . . . *hyena and wild boar*,' she resumed. '*In which case, Miss Fenton would be the first to agree that a fence is necessary; indeed, she would insist that one should be erected immediately, at the Hon. Emily Kaye's expense. She trusts, however, that this possibility is remote. As far as Miss Fenton herself is concerned, the only animal in her establishment is one Siamese cat which, during the ten years which Miss Fenton has owned it, has shown no inclination to stray into undesirable territories. . . .*'

She looked up again. 'I am not quite certain about "undesirable territories". It seems to make Emily's little garden sound rather too important.'

'I think I should just say "no inclination to stray".'

'But that is the end of the letter. And I should like it to end more emphatically.'

'It seems to me emphatic enough already.'

'You don't think I might add a sentence saying that this correspondence must now be regarded as closed?'

'But is it closed?'

'I wonder.' She sighed. I suspected that she would be bitterly disappointed if it were, though she could hardly say so to me. 'Let us *hope* it is closed,' she observed loftily. 'All so foolish, so petty, with so many beautiful things in the world.' She glanced at the letter once more. 'You're sure there's nothing else you would like me to take out? I hope not. I don't want to cut it too drastically.'

As I had only suggested the possibility of eliminating a few wild boar and hyena I felt that the implied reproof was unjustified.

'How will you sign it?' I asked.

'Ah! I'm glad you mention that point. I shall not sign it at all.'

I did not understand.

'Miss Perkins will sign my name for me.' (Miss Perkins was Rose's secretary. She was a beaky and faintly moustached lady who boasted that she was a direct descendant of the original Dorothy Perkins.)

'Yes,' she said, 'I think that will be best. Miss Perkins will sign for me. Underneath she will type "Dictated, but not signed, by Rose Fenton". That will give the whole affair a casual note. I would not like Emily to think that I was taking it too seriously.'

I could not suppress a sigh. It needed no very great effort of the imagination to realize the explosive effect which such a communication would have upon Miss Emily. And it needed no great experience of Miss Emily to be convinced that sooner or later — probably sooner — she would be descending upon me in fiery indignation, soliciting my support, and — unless I was very much mistaken — demanding that I should listen to a letter of her own. I should be obliged to do so, of course; to refuse would look like 'taking sides'.

But one thing I certainly would not do. I would not take Emily out to the water-garden. It was as peaceful as ever, the ripples were as soft as silk, and the shadows of the rushes moved across the water in a gentle saraband. But these delights appeared to have no power to soothe the savage breast of outraged femininity. I would keep Miss Emily indoors, and give her a strong cup of tea.

IV

The drama developed even more swiftly than I had anticipated. Rose must have posted her letter within an hour of coming to see me. I had hardly finished breakfast, on the following morning, before Gaskin announced the arrival of Miss Emily.

'I told her you were working,' he said, 'but she insisted. I've put her in the music room.'

I rose from the desk.

'If I were you,' said Gaskin severely, 'I'd let her wait.'

'I can't possibly let her wait.'

'You know what you are, if your morning's work is upset.'

'It would be much more upset if I didn't find out what she wanted.'

As soon as I opened the door of the music room, I knew the answer. It was war. This was proclaimed, not by any mystic symbols of garnets or moonstones, but by the steely glint in her eyes, and the ruthless stride with which she paced the carpet.

'I could not be more apologetic,' she announced, in vibrant tones which somehow seemed to contradict this statement. 'I feel quite *abject*, disturbing you like this.' The word 'abject' had the quality of a trumpet-note. 'About such a petty matter, too. Really, *too* petty.' Even the word 'petty' was invested with a sort of awful grandeur.

'I really do need advice,' she continued. 'A *man's* advice. When a woman is all alone, and when she is dealing with a dangerous lunatic . . .' She opened her bag and drew out a typed sheet of paper. 'An hour ago I received this. It is the most insulting letter from . . .' she gulped . . . 'from dear Rose.' The gulp, evidently, had been caused by the

216

effort of pronouncing the word 'dear'. She might have been swallowing a hot chestnut.

I felt that it was time to take a stand. 'I really don't think I ought to read it, if it's private.' There seemed no point in telling Miss Emily that I had already done so.

'No?' She paused for a moment, and then pushed the letter back. 'Perhaps it would be better not. But at least there can be no objection to giving you a general idea of its contents.'

'If you really feel. . . .'

'I certainly do.' She sat down firmly on the edge of the sofa and folded her arms. There was nothing for it but to listen.

'You may recall that last time you came to see me I happened to mention that my entire garden was being smothered by the seeds of the weeds blowing across from Rose's orchard. Yes?'

'I do seem to remember. . . .'

'Quite. And that there was some ridiculous complaint about my bonfire, and that you suggested we should toss up?'

'I'm afraid that may have been a mistake.'

'I am quite sure that it was a mistake. Not that I reproach you for it. Besides, if Rose had the faintest sense of fair play she would not hold me to such a bet. However, we must take her as she is, and I, for one, have no desire to go back on my word. If one gambles with people like Rose, one must take the consequences.

'Apart from that . . .' and here she rose, and began to pace the room again . . . 'I have other means at my disposal.'

This must be the cue for the entrance of the fence. Yes, here it came.

'I shall compel Rose to put up a fence,' she continued. 'That, at least, will keep out *some* of the weeds.'

In order to do so, I reflected, it would have to be higher than the Nelson Column.

'*Can* you compel Rose to put up a fence?'

This question seemed greatly to surprise Miss Emily. 'But of course. Why not?'

'I only wondered.'

'There is nothing to wonder about. There is already a fence in existence. It is her responsibility. She has allowed it to get into the most disgraceful state of repair. I am only asking her to fulfil her legal obligations — as I pointed out in my letter.'

'How did she reply?' I longed to know if Rose had kept in the bit about the hyena and the wild boar.

'You would hardly believe it, if I told you. It sounded like something written in a sort of delirium. There was a great deal about wild animals.'

'No? What sort of wild animals?'

'I hardly remember. Giraffes, bison . . . something like that.'

Rose must have changed it. I rather liked the giraffes.

'However, that was presumably Rose's idea of humour. There was nothing at all humorous about the general conclusion. She gave a blank refusal. She even has the temerity to suggest that no fence is necessary!'

'I suppose it *is* necessary?'

'Suppose?' Miss Emily gave something very like a snort. 'Really! Why should a fence ever have been put up at all if it were not necessary?'

I could not help thinking that this was not a very convincing retort. It seemed to me that a great many fences had been put up all over the world, in the long course of history, that were not necessary. Fences round nations, fences round property. They were supposed to be symbols of security, but they were cheating symbols. They had a precisely opposite effect from that which was intended. They did not prevent crime, they incited it; they led not to peace but to war. A world without fences would be a better world. However, that was anarchy, and I could not air such theories to Miss Emily, who was chairman of the local Conservatives Association.

So I merely murmured 'Quite.'

'There has been a fence there for over fifty years. My old gardener remembers it being put up. It was put up by the people on Rose's side of the boundary, and it was always maintained by them. Since Rose came, nothing has been done to it at all. It is all in bits and pieces — an *eyesore!*'

I recalled Rose's claim that the fence was totally invisible except from the top of Miss Emily's greenhouse. 'I suppose it stands out very much?' I asked, with assumed innocence.

Miss Emily looked at me sharply, as though she wondered if Rose had been prompting me. For a few seconds she hesitated. Then she said: 'At present some of it is partly concealed by a few laurels, but I am having those cut down.'

'Oh dear! That does seem a pity.'

'Not at all. They are diseased.' I was certain that Miss Emily was inventing this on the spur of the moment.

'Completely diseased, all of them,' she continued, with increasing heat. 'They must come down. Apart from that . . .' Again she hesitated. Then she looked over her shoulder, to make sure that she was not overheard. She lowered her voice. 'Apart from that I want to know what is going on.' She nodded mysteriously. 'It is not a pleasant thing to have to say about one of one's oldest friends — and I still look upon Rose as a friend — but I have a fancy that she is using those laurels to conceal the fact that she is *moving* the fence.'

'Moving it? Where?'

'Pushing it forward — little by little — into my property.'

This accusation greatly shocked me. Perhaps Miss Emily realized that she had gone too far, for she hastened on: 'Not that one can be *sure*, of course; it is not the sort of charge one would care to bring in a court of law. . . .'

'I should hope not.'

'All the same, it is a little strange that some of the palings appear to have found their way to *my* side of the ditch. They can hardly have been blown there by the wind. And one of the few remaining posts has *quite* obviously been tampered with. All very small and petty, of course, and I'm sure that if dear Rose wants a few extra feet of my land I should be only too happy to *give* them to her. I think my property is about the same size as hers — ('Half an acre smaller,' I thought, 'if she includes the gravel pit') — 'and the only reason why one always feels so strangely cramped in her garden is because it is perhaps not very well designed. However, she has to live with it, and I should be the last to offer her any advice . . . at least, till this foolish dispute is cleared up.'

'I do hope that it will be cleared up, without. . . .'

'Without going to law? I think we need have no fear of that. As soon as Rose understands the legal position, she is bound to see reason, and give way.'

'I suppose the legal position is quite clear?'

'Overwhelmingly.'

'Have your lawyers said so?'

She gave a superior smile. 'I should not dream of wasting money on lawyers in an affair like this. They would only tell me what I know already, that the law is on my side. Even if it were not, I should still fight, in the interests of common sense and common decency — not only for myself, but for all of us!'

I would have liked to ask her to what extent the other inhabitants of Meadowstream would benefit from the erection of a row of palings between her kitchen garden and Rose's orchard. However, there was a challenging ring in her voice which made it obvious that she saw herself in the role of champion of the oppressed, so I made no comment. After a few desultory remarks about the splendour of the weather — ('such golden days . . . one would have thought that they would have had a *mellowing* effect on people') — she rose to go. I saw her to the garden gate, and it was not till her car had vanished round the corner of the lane that I realized that she had forgotten to read me the reply which she had written to Our Rose. Perhaps, in view of what was to come, this was just as well.

CHAPTER XIV

ARMISTICE

IF ever Meadowstream had to elect a father confessor, there can be no doubt for whom we should vote. We should choose Marius. Not only because of his erudition, but because of his benignity. Whenever Marius is with us we are always on our best behaviour, not as children in the shadow of their schoolmaster — though we seldom leave him without learning something — but as adults in the presence of somebody whom we knew, instinctively, to be good. It is curious that so vague a quality as mere 'goodness', so difficult to define, should be so easy to recognize. It is like a light. If it is there, you see it instantly, and there is no argument about it. Virtue carries not only its own reward, but its own illumination.

So it was to Marius that I went, that afternoon, in order to see if there might be some means of halting the conflict between Miss Emily and Our Rose before it was too late. Even as I walked through the wood to his little house — a converted game-keeper's cottage, built in the style of

Victorian Gothic — I began to feel better. The wood was doing its well-known impersonation of a cathedral, with the beech trees acting as the columns, and traceries of green, flecked with September gold, serving the purpose of stained glass windows. The appropriate music for such a setting, I reflected, would be the Second Fantaisie of César Franck. For this is a piece in which Franck, whether by intention or by accident, created a *building*, of surpassing beauty, in sound. There are several noble themes, as solid and symmetrical as the vast structure of the cathedral itself, and through these themes filter subsidiary melodies of the most delicate colour — little echoes escaping through the gates of heaven.

Marius always took a long time to open the door, and as I stood in his porch I began to hum the opening bars to myself, in a rather wobbly bass. At last he came, and ushered me in. He never seemed surprised, at whatever hour one called. It was as though one were always expected, and welcome.

Nor did he ask me why I had come. Instead, after giving me a cigarette and lighting it with old-world courtesy, he walked to the window and said: 'It is almost incredible that he wrote it before breakfast.'

I was not prepared for this observation. 'Who? What?'

He turned in surprise. 'Your César Franck . . . was not that what you were humming? The Second Fantaisie?'

'My dear Marius, I had no idea that you knew it.'

'My dear Beverley' . . . and there was a note of mild indignation in his voice . . . 'there are moments when I am not entirely a musical Hottentot.'

This seemed an understatement, but I had no time to apologize, for he went on — with a reflective frown — 'Not that I agree with the popular conception of the Hottentots.

They have been greatly maligned. The sexual code of the Hottentots, for example, compares very favourably with the regulations of the Criminal Amendment Act. Would you not agree?'

'I can well believe it.'

He nodded gravely, and made a note on a piece of paper. 'But we were speaking of Franck, and the fact that he wrote that masterpiece before breakfast.'

'Why?'

Marius, as usual, managed to turn one's ignorance into a virtue. 'You are so musical,' he said, 'that you would probably have no patience for such trivial details. For people like myself they have an interest. It was simply because he was so poor that he had no alternative. He was obliged to spend most of his days giving music lessons. I think that is one of the major tragedies of history. There might have been another Symphony in D Minor. Instead of that, a dozen scruffy little Belgian children were taught to play the exercises of Stephen Heller when — in all probability — they would have been better employed in weeding the cabbage patch.'

He sighed and went over to the little harmonium which stood in the corner. He bent down to pull out a stop, and then straightened himself and shook his head. 'I was going to see if I could play the opening bars,' he said. 'But I think not. That piece needs a noble instrument. To play it on this would be like trying to make thunder on a tambourine.'

He turned abruptly. 'I am sure that you came to see me on some sort of business.'

'In a sense, yes. About Rose and Emily.'

'What have they been up to?'

'I'm afraid that a storm is brewing.'

Marius looked distressed. 'Another?' He sighed. 'Why

must they do it? Such amiable creatures, both of them, *au fond.* And indispensable to one another, if they only knew it. What is it this time?'

'It is a question of the fence between their two properties.'

'May I have the details?' He gave me an avuncular smile. 'Your details are always so vivid.'

'It is nice of you to say so.' I told him the story as well as I could remember it, bringing in as many details as possible, including Rose's hyena — or hyenas — and Miss Emily's accusation that Rose was lurking behind the laurels and pushing it forward into her property. When I had finished Marius got up and walked slowly to the window, where he stood tapping his fingers against the glass.

Then he turned. 'The thing which puzzles me,' he said, 'is the attitude of their legal advisers.'

'Which legal advisers?'

'Those whom they have presumably consulted. Why have their lawyers allowed things to get to such a pass?'

'But there haven't been any legal advisers.'

He stared at me incredulously. 'You mean to say that they have been writing these letters to each other, and making these extraordinary charges and counter-charges, without troubling to find out the legal position?'

'That is precisely what they have been doing.'

He took a deep breath. 'If it had not been said more than once before, I should be tempted to observe that women are incomprehensible.'

'What *is* the legal position?

'There is no legal position.'

'Marius, you are being tiresome.'

'I beg your pardon. That was not my intention. All I meant was that there is no sort of liability in common law for the owners of adjoining properties to fence either against or for the benefit of each other — except to prevent the straying of animals. Rose's hyenas were very much to the point.'

'So you mean that Emily hasn't a leg to stand on?'

'Quite.'

'But what about the question of precedent? Emily says there always has been a fence there. And she says that constitutes a legal precedent.'

'It does nothing of the sort. How can a legal precedent arise out of something which was not legal in the first instance?'

'Oh dear. It would kill poor Emily if she has to give way.'

'It would also kill poor Rose.'

'Marius, you must think of something. You always can if you try. If you don't, you'll have the death of two women on your hands.'

For a moment there was silence. Then I said: 'What about the weeds? Can't they be made to help in some way?'

'Not in the opinion of the second Lord Coleridge.'

'What are you talking about?'

'Forgive me . . . I was forgetting that you did not study law. I was referring to the case of *Giles* v. *Walker*, in the Queen's Bench Division in August 1890 . . . or was it 1891? One's memory is a sieve. But at least I recall the principle that was established.'

'What did Giles do to Walker?'

'Nothing. That was the whole point. He claimed damages from Walker for allowing thistledown from his fields to blow over on to his land. Lord Coleridge dismissed the claim with some sharpness. I remember his words. "No reasoning man," he said, "would venture to demand damages for such natural accidents. It would be tantamount to suing Dame Nature herself." '

'Oh dear! If Rose knew about that, poor Emily would never hear the last of it.' And, indeed, it was only too easy to imagine how Our Rose would turn such information to account. I could hear her purring accents: '*Dear* Emily . . . taking legal action against the Universe! Poor darling, deluded thing . . . sending writs to the moon, and bringing injunctions against the wind!' It was all quite terrible to contemplate, and my mind was torn between pity for Miss Emily's humiliation and horror at the thought of Rose's triumph.

Suddenly Marius clapped his hand to his forehead. 'What a fool I am! I had forgotten the Ministry of Agriculture!'

'How does the Ministry of Agriculture come into it?'

'It was precisely because of Lord Coleridge's judgment that the Ministry passed certain regulations compelling people to clean their land of weeds. It is a tiresome business, and it involves the issuing of a writ, but it can be done. Will you forgive me? I would like to do some telephoning.'

He disappeared into his study and shut the door, leaving me staring at the heap of letters in the tray on his desk. I longed to read them. Is that immoral? Probably, but I can never see other people's letters without itching to know their contents. Marius's letters looked especially fascinating. Many of the envelopes bore foreign stamps. The top one was from the British Embassy in Teheran, and was marked Highly Confidential. Was Marius a secret service agent? Nobody ever seemed to know. Perhaps, if I strolled over quite casually, and took a hasty peep. . . .

However, I was saved from succumbing to temptation by the return of Marius, with a look of triumph on his face. He had consulted the Ministry of Agriculture and it appeared that there were indeed quite a number of regulations in Miss Emily's favour, so that if she persisted, she could oblige Our Rose to bend the knee.

'A most fortunate position,' he commented. 'They both have the law on their sides.'

'But mightn't that make it worse? Mightn't they go ahead and destroy each other?'

'Not if we play our cards cleverly. They must never learn that they are both right; they must only be convinced that they are both wrong. Emily must never know that she has the power to make Rose cut down her weeds. She must only know that she has no power to make her put up a fence. Rose must never know that Emily cannot make her put up a fence. She must only know that Emily can compel her to cut down her weeds. As soon as they are convinced of these facts, they will both beat a hasty retreat.'

'Marius, you really are a genius. But how are they to be convinced?'

He gave me a sly glance. 'You have a very persuasive tongue.'

I sat up sharply. 'No. I should be quite the wrong person. I should get everything mixed up. They wouldn't believe a word I said, even if I said it right. You must do it. At once. This afternoon.'

He sighed. Then he walked over to the tray of letters and turned one or two of them over. 'I had been hoping to deal with some arrears of correspondence,' he said. 'However, perhaps the *affaire* Rose-Emily should take precedence.'

That, I thought, was noble of him. It showed a proper sense of values. The Highly Confidential letter from the Embassy in Teheran was probably only concerned with some disputed frontier, and if Marius delayed answering it, the result would only be, at worst, the loss of a few million pounds' worth of oil fields. Whereas Miss Emily's fence and Rose's weeds were urgent, vital realities, affecting the lives of us all.

II

Marius must have gone to work with great speed, and also with great determination, because that very evening the telephone rang twice in rapid succession. Both Rose and Emily desired to see me without delay. Had I a moment before going to bed? Yes, I said, I had. I had ten minutes at eight, and another ten minutes at nine. I had, in fact, the whole evening, but I did not want the two ladies to meet each other.

Rose was the first of the ladies to be received. We sat in the little courtyard, which was looking absurdly romantic in the fading light, but Rose was not in the mood to expiate upon its poetic charms. She was in a state of considerable agitation, and plunged into the heart of the matter without any preliminaries.

'I felt you should be the first to know that I have written today to Emily to tell her that I should be delighted to cut down the weeds in my orchard, and also, if she still feels so strongly about it, to erect a fence between our two properties.'

This startling information came out at top speed in a single, prolonged gulp, and as she delivered it Rose's face was contorted in a manner that suggested she was having a tooth extracted.

'I can see you are surprised,' she observed, pecking at a leaf of rose geranium, and sniffing it nervously.

'Yes, I am rather.' I had expected that there might be an uneasy truce, but I had not anticipated such an abject surrender. 'Have you been taking legal advice?'

She gazed at me with great innocence. 'Advice? Oh no! Why should you think that?'

'I wondered if perhaps you had been discussing it with . . . with anybody.'

She shook her head emphatically. 'Certainly not. It is true that dear Marius called this afternoon, and I may perhaps have mentioned something about it to him — I really can hardly remember. If I did — and it is quite possible — I have no doubt that he would have given me excellent advice.'

I interpreted this cryptic remark as meaning that Marius had waved a copy of the Ministry of Agriculture's statute about weeds in her face.

'However, when one is with Marius one does not bother about such petty matters. We talked of very different things, and as usual, I learnt much from him. Such wisdom — such serenity! When he had gone I felt quite, quite differently about the whole affair.'

I felt that this, at least, was true.

'So I sat down,' she continued, 'and thought of poor Emily, and her little troubles, and how agitated she was becoming, and how bad it was not only for her, but for all of us, that there should be hostile vibrations. . . .'

Here it comes, I thought. And indeed it did. For Rose had manœuvred herself into an argumentative position in which she was immune from attack.

'Vibrations,' she repeated, and proceeded to ride her favourite hobby-horse. Hostile vibrations, she assured me — not for the first time — were like the ripples in a village pond. Throw in a single stone of discord, and they would spread out in ever widening circles. Emily, it seemed, was the stone of discord, and the only way to counter her influence was to send out vibrations in a different direction. At this point Rose's simile became somewhat confused, for it was obvious that one set of ripples meeting another set would lead, not to calm, but to agitation. However she rose, as it were, triumphantly from her pond, her eyes glistening with goodwill.

'Yes,' she breathed. 'Emily shall have her little fence. And I hope, I do indeed, that every time she sees it she will be reminded of the spirit in which it was erected. Not that this will be often, for — as I think I told you — it will be almost totally invisible from any point except the roof of her conservatory.' A certain sharpness crept into her voice, but she checked it quickly, and continued to glisten.

'As for the weeds . . .' She shrugged her shoulders. 'In view of the fact that there is only a very small patch to be scythed, and that most of the "weeds" consist of a bed of specimen lupins which I was saving for their seed . . .' She paused as a thought struck her. 'It might be a good idea to have some of them specially packeted, and to send them to her with my lŏve. And then, when they came up, I could call one day and admire them, and tell her — quite casually — that they were the weeds to which she had so greatly objected.' She glistened more than ever at the thought of this admirable revenge. 'It might make her feel rather foolish. It *might* . . . but then, of course, it might not. Dear Emily has a great deal to learn.'

She rose to her feet. 'But there . . . I am keeping you from your work. How amused you must be by these tea-cup tragedies!' She gave a sharp peck at my sleeve. 'May I make a rather naughty suggestion?'

What could be coming now? I sincerely trusted that Rose was not going to propose — as she had once done — that we should dance bare-foot on the lawn.

She leant forward, her eyes gleaming, and echoing the cool fire of the moonstone necklace. 'I really think,' she whispered, 'that one of these days you should put dear Emily in a book!'

And then, with an extra tinkle in her laughter, she was gone.

III

Punctually at nine o'clock Miss Emily arrived. She, too, was 'received' in the courtyard. I was beginning tọ feel like some odd sort of Eastern potentate, deciding the fate of nations — though, in fact, I had really played no active part in the conflict; it was only thanks to Marius that we had no murder on our hands.

Miss Emily, like Our Rose, plunged straight into the heart of the matter. And she, too, announced her news with considerable facial distortion, as though she were suffering from acute indigestion.

'I should like you to know,' she said, 'that I have decided to take no further action in the matter I discussed with you this morning. I shall not insist that Rose puts up a fence. Nor shall I insist that she cuts down her weeds.' She took a deep breath. 'I could, of course, if I chose. But I do not choose.'

She looked me straight in the eyes as she made this pronouncement. I was glad that the light was so dim, because I could not pretend to be surprised. I am no good at assuming expressions which I do not feel. When I tell a lie it is almost as though a gun went off. I do not claim this as a virtue, I admit it as a misfortune.

'I am so glad to hear it. I am sure it is for the best.'

'Quite.'

'What made you come to this decision?'

She shrugged her shoulders. 'I hardly know.' She paused for a moment. 'No. Perhaps that is not quite true. I think what really made me change my mind is that I could not bear the idea of making poor Rose look ridiculous. Does that sound very priggish of me?'

I should have liked to remark that it sounded, not

priggish, but highly mendacious. However, my role was that of peacemaker.

'After all,' she continued, 'I *am* very fond of the poor thing. I should be really distressed if I were obliged to put her in a humiliating position.'

'I see. I thought, perhaps, that you might have been taking new advice.'

She raised her eyebrows. 'Really? Why should I seek advice?'

'I was just wondering.'

'I have come to this decision entirely of my own accord. In fact, I have discussed this matter with nobody but yourself.'

'I see.'

It is possible that I did not appear entirely convinced, for she suddenly seemed to recollect something. 'Wait . . . I may have mentioned it . . . *en passant*, of course . . . to that charming friend of yours, Marius.'

'Oh — have you been seeing Marius?'

'He happened to call this afternoon.'

'What did he have to say about it?'

'About the fence?' She laughed lightly. 'Really, I'm sure I have no idea. I could hardly be sure if he said anything at all. He may have done, of course. If he did, it was doubtless to the point.'

'I'm sure it was.'

'But when one is in contact with a brain of such intelligence, one does not waste time in discussing such trivialities.'

I translated this as meaning that Marius had given her a very terse résumé of the common law.

'As far as I am concerned the whole matter is completely forgotten. I shall put Rose and her weeds out of my mind.'

'Won't that be rather difficult?'

'Not at all, if one has any strength of character.'

'But if you are taking down your laurel hedge. . . .'

'Oh — the laurels!' She gave a rather forced laugh. 'I shall not be cutting them after all.'

'I thought they were diseased?'

'Not nearly so badly as I had imagined. I have been out to have another look at them.'

'What was the matter with them?'

She blinked rapidly. 'A form of fungus. Quite common, I believe, in this hot weather. Only a few branches affected.'

'Then it is peace? And we can all relax?'

She managed a smile, and rose to her feet. 'One can only hope so. Of course, with Rose, one never knows. She *may* take this gesture as a sign of weakness. You saw how she was about my little bonfire. She wanted to stop me having one at all. However, that would be something which I really could *not* tolerate. If one's property is knee-deep in weeds from somebody else's garden, I cannot believe that the law does not allow one at least to burn them. I try to behave like a Christian but I do not aim to be a martyr.'

She extended her hand. 'Such a wonderful night,' she sighed. 'So many stars! Such a moon! One can see the face of the lady of the moon quite clearly. It always seems to remind me of somebody I know, but I can never quite think of whom.'

I stared up at the golden disc. Yes, the lady of the moon was standing out, embossed in shadow, in vivid outline. She reminded me, too, of somebody I knew. It was strange that Miss Emily did not recognize her, for obviously it was Our Rose. From her lofty eminence she was smiling. Perhaps it was an omen.

Time would show.

CHAPTER XV

POT-POURRI

I HAVE called this chapter 'Pot-Pourri' because in every gardener's year there are a thousand small excitements and delights which fit into no general pattern and fall under no specific heading, and it seems a pity that those pleasures should be lost. In the same way I find it difficult to leave a rose-bed without gathering up the freshly fallen petals; there is something not only wasteful but callous in leaving those fragments of gold and crimson velvet to wither in the sun.

The ingredients with which we can fill such a bowl of memories are many and various. We might begin with some inventions. I have invented a great many things over the years, and though they have no great scientific merit, they have one quality which makes them, perhaps, superior to the inventions of the scientists. None of them explodes. None of them makes even the smallest bang. This, surely, is a point in their favour. Were I President of the Institute of Inventions — or whatever it is called — whenever anybody brought along anything new, the first question I should ask him would be: 'Does it explode?' If he said yes, it did, I should show him to the door.

High up on the list of my non-explosive inventions is the . . .

NICHOLS BEE-LURING DEVICE FOR THE PAINLESS REMOVAL OF BEES FROM WINDOW PANES

If you are fond of bees — and really it would seem almost impossible not to be fond of them — you will admit that in spite of the music that they make and the delicacies that they manufacture, they are, on occasions, a bore. Bumble bees, for example, seem positively to glue themselves to dahlias, and there is also a small brown bee that attaches itself to the blossoms of scabious as if by suction. These bees greatly hinder the picking of mixed bunches in the summer, unless, of course, you are a Hun, who flicks them off with a callous finger. Even more bothersome are those fussy, bustling bees who obviously resent one's presence in the herbaceous border at all, or — which is worse — decide that one is picking the flowers specially for their benefit, and buzz round the bunch all the way across the lawn, and even follow one into the house. These bees cause hours of work, for they have to be painfully removed from the window pane and transported back to the garden.

It is to solve this major problem that the NICHOLS BEE-LURING DEVICE has been invented.

What you do is this. You take an empty match-box, and open it, and stalk up to the window, where the bee is stuck to the glass, gazing sadly at the garden from which it has been banished. You then clamp the open match-box over the bee. There will be furious protests, and wild beatings of wings, but you must steel yourself against these manifestations. This is a case where you must be cruel to be kind. If you drop the match-box and let the bee buzz off, it will only stun itself on the chandelier, and then you will have to turn out the cats and call for Gaskin and the whole day will be ruined.

No . . . you must put the open match-box firmly over the bee, with one swift, incisive stroke. Then, turning a deaf ear to the sounds of rage inside, you must slowly close the match-box. This, I warn you, is agony. There is always a terrible chance that a small piece of bee may be squeezed in the match-box . . . a wing bruised or a leg dislocated or something equally deplorable. You have to take that risk. And really, if you are careful, the risk is small. In all my bee-removing life, I can only recall one casualty, which was a bumble-bee of exceptional girth and stupidity . . . who, in addition, was obviously and aggressively tight.

Then you take the buzzing match-box to the open door, and gently release it. Out flies a brown, dazed creature — hovers for a second in bewilderment — and then arrows its way through the free air, to the sky and the trees and the distant flowers.

Please remember the Nichols Bee-Luring Device. No patent has been applied for. It is among my gifts to mankind.

II

There are even pleasanter inventions in store. For the next one I claim no credit at all. It comes from Miss Mint, and it has a very simple title. It is called . . .

THE LAVENDER FAN

I love fans, in all shapes, sizes, materials and designs.

No poet, to my recollection, has contrived a lyric worthy of this device. I wonder why? In the folds of a fan, surely, a flock of poems must be sleeping, to be evoked by a gentle flutter of the pen.

Miss Mint evoked such a poem for me, one evening in June, when I had gone over to see her about a Sale of Work. Miss Mint is one of that gentle army of countrywomen to whom a Sale of Work is an event of some importance, to be taken seriously. Such women receive small thanks, and if the great world ever thinks of them at all it is with a smile of patronizing indulgence. In the popular esteem they are a collection of well-meaning old maids, who have nothing better to do than stand in village halls trying to sell each other their home-made pickles and tea-cosies and bed-socks. That is one way of looking at them. Another is to regard them as a band of women — none of them rich, many of them old, and all of them tired — who work themselves to a standstill, cooking and sewing and knitting and bottling, in order to help a local church which is still a reality in their lives. Such women do not make the headlines, and nobody is ever likely to interview them on television. But in the fabric of the national life they are a thread of gold.

As I walked up the stone-flagged path of Miss Mint's cottage, I wondered what her own contribution to the sale would be. She had no lumber-room in which to rummage; her governess's pension left her with little to spare, and yet she always contrived to produce some object for which there was a ready market. I was soon to know. After she had received my own small contributions — with the usual bird-like sounds of delighted gratitude — I asked her what she was taking to the sale herself.

'Just some little things I have made,' she said, with the usual pretty flush that always came on the rare occasions when she talked about herself. 'They are not much . . . but I thought, perhaps . . . do you think a shilling each would be too much to ask?'

'But, Miss Mint, I do not know what they are.'

She laughed and shook her head at her own foolishness. 'I will show you one of them.'

She walked over to the old walnut bureau, and drew out an object wrapped in tissue paper, loosely tied with white ribbon.

'I know you love undoing parcels,' she said, as she handed it to me.

I undid the ribbon. The tissue paper fell away. There in my hand was the fan, from which there floated a delicate fragrance.

'But this is enchanting,' I said.

'Do you think it would be too much if we asked a shilling each?'

'It would be far too little. You should ask half a crown.'

'Oh, I don't think as much as *that*. They are very easy to make. Just some lavender, a piece of starched muslin, some ribbon, and some coloured wool. You see, the lavender is inside the muslin, so that when you wave the fan, the scent comes out. Let me show you.'

I will condense Miss Mint's rather discursive explanation into four simple stages.

1. Pick a bunch of the lavender, with nice long stalks, because the stalks form the handle.

2. Cut out two pieces of starched muslin, lay the lavender between them, with the stalks protruding, and sew the muslin together.

3. Bind the stalks with lavender-coloured ribbon, and tie a bow.

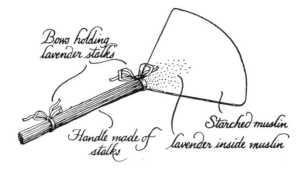

4. To make the fan even prettier, crochet a design of lavender on the outside. This is simplicity itself, because lavender is so easy to draw; you merely make a lot of blue strokes going up, and one green stroke going down. Thus:

So there we are. I hope you will agree that Miss Mint's invention is worth while. Indeed, I would go further than that, and suggest that it is important. The world needs lavender fans a great deal more urgently than it needs many of the things which it regards as essential. At every international conference there should be lavender fans, to waft sweetness into the dilated nostrils of the participants. There should be lavender fans on the table at every director's meeting, and there should be a large stock of lavender fans at the entrances to the House of Commons and Congress. Dr. Edith Summerskill should be provided with a lavender fan of such vast dimensions and such overpowering sweetness that she would be weighed down by it, and drugged into a kindly stupor, in which she would be incapable of talking any more nonsense. Indeed, all the bores of the world should be compulsorily equipped with lavender fans. But the nice people should have them, too, to perfume the passing hour.

III

My next invention has a rather flamboyant title. It is called

THE COURTYARD OF ETERNAL FLOWERS.

If that sounds like a scene from an old-fashioned pantomime, I really do not care. I like scenes from old-fashioned pantomimes.

The germ of the idea was given to me, quite inadvertently, by Our Rose. It was a very hot afternoon in August, and as I walked down her herbaceous border, I was astonished — and slightly sickened — to discover a superb clump of immaculate *lilium auratum*. Astonished, because they were in full sun, whereas *lilium auratum* prefer semi-shade, and sickened, because mine had been battered by a violent thunderstorm. When I expressed my surprise, Rose babbled her usual nonsense about 'vibrations', as though she had some secret powers which softened the rays of the sun and blunted the teeth of the storm. To cut a very long story very short, I afterwards discovered that the auratums had been planted in biscuit tins, in the richest possible soil, and kept in a sheltered shady yard until they were in bud, after which they had been transplanted — biscuit tins and all — to the border. So much for Rose's 'vibrations'.

However, I bear no malice, because it was through Rose's gross deceit and cunning that I hit upon one of the happiest ideas in my whole life of gardening.

You remember the little courtyard outside the music room? It is thirty feet square, with a small pool in the middle, in which there stands a pleasantly bloated cupid holding up a cup which is supposed to spout, and would, if I had not had a row with the Water Rate people. This courtyard is paved with York stone, in which there are about twenty pockets for flowers. Like most of such places it was a source of delight, but it was also a source of frustration. When one of the pockets had finished flowering — well, it had finished flowering, and there was nothing to be done about it. For the remaining eleven months of the year there was only a square patch of empty leaves or fading stalks. You longed to plant something else, but how? You couldn't plant a cluster of lobelia on top of a cluster of aubretia; both would die. You longed to lift out the aubretias, but then there would be no aubretias next spring, which would be a most gruesome prospect. So you couldn't lift out the aubr. . . .

Suddenly, just like that, in the middle of a word as it were, I realized that you *could* lift out the aubr . . . etias. Rose, with her deceit, her Oriental cunning, had shown the way. Biscuit tins! That was the answer. Not common or garden biscuit tins, of course — a much superior variety. Boxes of galvanized iron, with holes punched in the bottom for drainage. Boxes which could be filled with soil as rich and delicate as cocoa. Boxes made to fit, to the fraction of an inch, the pocket which they were destined to occupy.

It was the most wonderful idea, and it came to me at about four-thirty on a stormy afternoon in late November. (The reader will agree that the precise details of such an important historical discovery should be preserved for posterity.) There was not a moment to lose. Darkness was gathering apace, and the village ironmonger's would soon be shutting. I hustled into an overcoat, ran across the lawn to the garage, and hurtled down the lane at an indecorous

NIGHT

pace, wondering why it was that all my gardening career seemed to have to be conducted at top speed.

The people at the ironmonger's were charming but dense. No; perhaps that is not fair. It was not the fault of the girl behind the counter, who was only 'obliging', that she could not instantly produce eighteen galvanized iron boxes, punched for drainage, cut into an assortment of special shapes. She did her best. She waved a fish-scoop in the air, and she produced a device of perforated tin, which had something to do with steaming cod. But she ended up by saying that perhaps it might be better to 'have them made'.

Well, I did have them made. That was a story of yet more struggle and adventure, which must wait for some other time. All that need immediately concern the reader — which means you, if you hanker after eternally flori-ferous courtyards — is that the boxes cost only twelve shillings apiece and that they have been an unqualified success.

For example, I am writing these words at the end of February. If it were not for the boxes there would be no flowers in the courtyard at all. As it is, there are quite a number, for only yesterday I carried five of the boxes out of the cold frame, and set them in their appointed pockets. Here are the contents of those boxes.

Number One is thickly planted with miniature daffodils, only a few inches high, but of a gold so radiant that they seem to be creating their own sunshine. Round the edges of this box I had set hardy maidenhair ferns, so that they should not look too formal. Needless to say, if the daffodils had not been in the frame, they would not have been in flower for another month. Apart from that, without the magic box I should not have been able to have them in the courtyard at all. I could not have spared the space.

Number Two is equally thickly planted with *galanthus elwesii*, which is the aristocrat of all snowdrops. These were not kept in the frame, for that would have made them bloom too early. They are edged with nice green chunks of moss, which looks as if it were actually growing on the grey stones.

Number Three is just a formal square of one of the earliest crocuses . . . Tomasinianus. These have been in the frame, but only for three weeks, to bring them on. In the rich soil in which they are planted they have grown into much finer specimens than if they had been naturalized in the grass. Also, they have not been pecked by the birds.

Number Four is filled with blue and white grape hyacinths. (By some strange mischance, it was only a year ago that I learned about white grape hyacinths. They are even more enchanting than the blue ones, but I think they look best together.)

Number Five is a most charming mixture of scillas, winter aconites and chionodoxas, which looks like a bouquet that someone has left lying on the pavement. I am afraid that the aconites will be over before the others, but that does not really matter, as their leaves are so pretty.

So there we are. February 27th is the date, it is full winter, the wind is in the north-east and the sky is the colour of dirty linen. But through my window I look out on to spring.

IV

Those are three of the major inventions that go into my pot-pourri of gardening. There are, of course, a host of others. There is, for example, the important discovery that if you pick a bunch of Christmas roses, and then pick a few tips of Lawson cypress, and arrange the cypress tips behind the Christmas roses *inside out*, the result is of a beauty indescribable. Because, you see, the inside of the Lawson cypress, which forms the commonest hedge in a million suburban gardens, is delicately flecked with silver. When you put it behind the Christmas roses, the white and the silver seem to sing together. It is moonlight calling to moonlight.

However, the pot-pourri bowl is not composed only of inventions. It contains surprises, mysteries, and things that happen by accident. Such as a certain fantastic moss that suddenly appeared on a shelf of the greenhouse, flourished for a season, and then died away, never to return. This moss seemed to be composed of thousands of tiny palm trees. They were so small that you could have planted a dozen of them on a sixpenny piece; in spite of this, the palm-tree illusion was complete. Being an inveterate 'shrinker', I used to go out to the greenhouse and bend low over them and transport myself to a green desert, and ride about among them on an imaginary camel . . . which, you must admit, was an exhilarating and inexpensive form of entertainment. I even went up to the British Museum Library and tried to find out what sort of moss it was. This was less exhilarating. I do not recommend a trip to the British Museum Library, on a hot summer afternoon, in search of rare mosses. After a while one begins to feel strangely like one of the rare mosses oneself. Apart from that, if one does not fill in the form very clearly, one is presented at the end of several hours with an astonishing number of books about the prophet Moses.

Moments of delight go into the bowl — such as the morning in May when I woke up late, with the sun high in the heavens, and a warm, gentle breeze ruffling the drawn blinds. For a few seconds I did not realize that there was any particular reason for excitement; and then I suddenly realized that through the window was drifting a faint fragrance of wistaria blossom. It had happened at last, as I had planned it seven years before. All through those seven years I had been training the wistaria towards my window, balancing on ladders in a high wind, hammering nails into the old chimney stack, twisting the new shoots along wires in directions which they did not wish to follow. (Wistaria is very temperamental and perverse when you try to train it, and unless it is handled with the utmost delicacy it bruises and dies off.)

And now, here it was; I shall never forget jumping up and hurrying to the window and leaning out to greet it. The sprays of blossom were already warm in the sun, and they were reaching up to the ledge as though they were trying to climb inside. If you leaned out, you could follow the course of the branches right down the side of the house till they plunged into the ground, far away at the corner of the south wall. It was marvellous to think of the long distance they had travelled, and still more marvellous that through every inch of that journey they had born in their veins the magic coloured dyes and perfumed essences which were now trembling into bloom.

But we must not overcrowd our bowl with casual memories, or there will be no room left for certain ingredients which are essential in this very personal pot-pourri. Therefore, without any further ado, I will write down the words. . . .

FIR CONES

V

I have such a love of Scotch pines that psychiatrists would probably find it pathological. I love the smell of them, the look of them, the feel of them, and the sound of them. A schoolboy hero of mine — (his name, I remember, was J. C. Tanner; he had a snub nose, sandy hair, and a twisted smile) — wrote me a letter, the day before he was killed on active service, which contained a poem about pines. One line drifts back to me, over the years . . . '*They catch the echo of the distant seas.*' Not great poetry, just a trite observation in a young reporter's notebook. But the line still moves me. I used to stand under those trees, after his death, clutching that letter, listening to those distant seas. I still do.

If you have read any other books of mine, you will find a great many Scotch pines, here, there and everywhere, sprouting up in all sorts of unexpected pages. My young couples always seem to stray into their shadows, in moments of crisis. My magic casements — or such as I have endeavoured to contrive — open not on to perilous seas, but on to high dark branches, through which the wind swirls like the sea on a rocky coast. I have an *idée fixe* — psychiatrists please note — that it would be pleasing to die to the sound of the wind sighing through the branches of a pine which oneself had planted. That is why, beneath my bedroom at Merry Hall, there is a rather feeble pine which I brought back in a sponge-bag from Austria. While I was digging it up I could hear the cow-bells in the valley far below — tinkle, tinkle, sharp and treble, like a passage from an unwritten page of *Rosenkavalier*. 'The sound of those bells,' I said to myself 'will somehow creep into the sap of this little tree.' Tinkle, tinkle, sharp and treble. 'This thin sweet music will never die. I shall hear it always. Maybe I shall make other people hear it, too.' With which Shakespearian resolve, I thrust the tree into the sponge bag . . . from which it was frequently dragged, during the next few days, by a series of bewildered customs officials. But it survived. It grows higher and higher. Tinkle, tinkle, sharp and treble. Well . . . you *have* heard the music, haven't you? But it was of the cones that I intended to write. One of the most exciting moments, if you have planted a lot of Scotch firs, is when they first begin to grow fir cones. You feel at once exhilarated and alarmed. Exhilarated, because it proves that they really *are* Scotch firs, and are doing their stuff, and are producing these charming objects for your special delight — smooth green cones which will eventually grow brown, and swell, and fan out. Alarmed, because you feel that they may be taxing their strength, like Indian child-wives who produce babies before they have reached their teens. So you rush indoors for a safety razor blade, and come out again, and slice off cone after cone, and cone after cone, till suddenly you feel that really nothing could be more boring, and that you must let Nature take its course.

I will add a practical footnote to this rhapsody. There is only one disadvantage to Scotch firs — an odious little worm that attacks the tender new shoots every year. You walk out, on a bright June morning, with the intention of measuring the new growth, and smacking your lips over the way they are reaching up to the heavens, and suddenly, to your horror, you notice that a number of them are wilting. Close inspection reveals a sheer tragedy; at the base of the stem they are bleeding resin, and if you scrape away the resin you find a hole, and out of the hole pops this quite deplorable worm, which glares at you like one of the nastiest creatures Disney ever created. You squash it, of course — not without nausea — for its body proves to be filled with a loathsome sort of yellow custard. But in all probability the harm has already been done; the new sprout fades and dies; and you have lost a whole year's growth.

So what do you do? You do this. You buy a tin of nicotine powder, and you buy a thing called a powder blower, and on the second week in August you go out and puff the powder all over the trees in a thin cloud. It is a tedious operation, and if there is the slightest wind, the powder blows up your nose and makes you sneeze and — in all probability — starts several deadly diseases which will kick you off at the age of sixty. But sixty is a long way ahead, and, in the meantime, the powder totally destroys the worm. Please be careful, however, not to leave any of it on the lower branches, where the cats might get at it.

VI

THE MOONFLOWER

In the long list of exotics with which, at various times, I have experimented — often with small success — the moonflower comes very near the top; not only because I have at last brought it to bloom, in all its luminous beauty, but because it has so consistently eluded me over the years, like a will-o'-the-wisp in a summer garden.

It is a flower of the night — and of only a single night. It opens when the sun has sunk behind the hills. No butterfly has ever lighted upon it — it keeps its sweetness for the moths. At dawn it falters, and in the rays of the morning it fades and shrivels. And yet, in its few hours of exquisite existence, it is strangely hardy and resilient. One evening I picked a bunch of moonflowers and arranged them in a ruff of lace paper; then I took them to London, to a dancer's dressing-room. There they glittered, in the stuffy little room, under the hot lights of the make-up table, while the last melancholy phrases of *Swan Lake* drifted from the distance. When she came in, and took them, and held them to her bosom, I had the satisfaction of feeling that I had contrived, for a moment, a perfect picture — the white flowers, the white dress, the white skin. The moonflowers might have been designed for the Swan Princess and for Tchaikowski's music. They lasted, so she told me, till the dawn, firm and radiant, and they died dramatically as she went to bed. They must have the theatre in their blood.

These romantic blossoms could come within your grasp, if Diana smiles upon you, and if — which is perhaps rather more important — you follow certain elementary rules about temperature and compost. So let me tell you more about them.

I saw my first moonflowers in southern India, during the war; they were climbing up the columns of a ruined Hindu temple on the outskirts of Madras. They had a cool, intrinsic innocence against a background which was dark and troubling. In form they resembled the simple wild convolvulus of the hedgerows, but they had a span of three or four inches, and their whiteness was faintly phosphorescent, with a hint of the palest green, such as one glimpses in the fire of a glow-worm. Their fragrance could not be caught in words, but to me it suggested a blend of incense and the peel of fresh lemons.

I gathered some seeds and eventually took them home. Three weeks later they were blown up by the Luftwaffe, with the rest of my possessions. That was the end of Act One.

Act Two came some years later when I sat down to write the first chapter of a detective novel called *The Moonflower*. It bore this title because it was through the germination of a moonflower seed that my detective discovered the identity of the murderer.

As I say, I sat down and wrote

251

THE MOONFLOWER

A Novel
by
Beverley Nichols

CHAPTER I

(This is by far the most pleasant moment in writing a book; and it is not repeated until, some months later, one writes the word 'Finis', and collapses in a heap over the desk.)

At precisely this moment Gaskin entered with the mail. Any excuse is good enough to stop writing a novel, so I began to open the letters. At the top was a bulky letter from the Argentine. It was from a reader unknown to me, and it contained a dozen seeds of the moonflower. One would hardly have been human if one had not taken this as a favourable omen. The next few days were much occupied with these seeds; three of them I nicked with a razor-blade, three I soaked in luke-warm water, three I allowed to bask in the sun — it was mid-May — three I planted in a sheltered spot beneath the balustrade. But alas, it was a grey, wet summer, and only one of the plants survived. It struggled to a height of four feet, never flowered, and fell to an early frost. End of Act Two.

Act Three is laid in Jamaica, whither I went, on the following winter, to stay with an old friend who was once one of the uncrowned kings of the world of fashion — Edward Molyneux. My aeroplane landed just before dawn, and I drove up to a white, silent villa, overlooking a sea whose waves were just beginning to be flecked with silver. It seemed absurd to go to bed, so I walked out into the sleeping garden, and there I found the moonflowers waiting for me, hundreds and hundreds of them, rioting over a low white wall that surrounded the swimming pool. Every moment it grew lighter, and this was their hour of greatest loveliness, when they were still intoxicated with the secrets of the night. They made me think of young girls in white dresses, dancing out of a candle-lit ballroom — dancing out on to the lawn to the strains of the last waltz, in the cool of the morning.

I had travelled a long way, and the journey had not been easy. Ten days of gales in the Atlantic, a blizzard in Bermuda, a tornado in Nassau, and on the final flight to Jamaica, one of the engines had failed. But it was worth it. The moonflowers made up for everything. When I tore myself away from them and went to find my bedroom, there was an airmail letter from England on the dressing-table, containing the first reviews of my novel, which had just been published. They were very gratifying reviews. I had been right in thinking that the omens were favourable.

So ended Act Three, but the play goes on. For I came home with several hundred seeds, and this time I took no chances. The first problem was to try to duplicate the soil of Jamaica, which was basically volcanic with a plentiful overlay of decayed tropical vegetable matter. I could not contrive an eruption in the Home Counties, but I could, and did, compound various mixtures of sand, gravel, leaf-mould and peat. (The grittiest mixtures were the most successful.) The first seeds were sown in mid-March in the conservatory, at a temperature of fifty. (I imagine that you could probably sow them, with success, on the window-ledge of any warm living-room.) They germinated in six weeks, and were set out at the beginning of May. This was too soon; none of them flowered. The main crop came from seeds sown two months later, and planted out at the end of

June. The first flower came on July 23rd, and till the end of September they were a source of enchantment. I would like to say — as Our Rose would certainly have said — that they were 'a positive mass, my dear', but that would not be true. There were never more than a dozen on a single night. But what did that matter? I cannot tell you what it feels like to come home, on a night of midsummer, to open a door in a garden wall, to cross the moonlit lawn, and to find these unearthly blossoms waiting for you. They hang on the balustrade in chains of silver stars, breathing fragrance. Like all things beautiful, they evoke other forms of beauty, in a different medium. The beauty of the moon-flower evokes music — the nocturnes of Chopin, the preludes of Debussy, and, above all, the long, haunting cadences of *Swan Lake*. You can hardly ask for more, from a little brown seed.

VII

The pot-pourri bowl is not big enough. As soon as I have finished with one memory, a host of others come flocking up, like the rooks which at this moment are wheeling across Mrs. Maples's field, on their way to the distant pine-woods. I should like to put something about those rooks into the bowl, for Marius once told me many strange tales about their habits; and their raucous cries, to me, make a wild, compelling music . . . the same sort of music which tugs at the heart of a Scotsman when he hears the bagpipes.

But the bowl is full, and there is no room for the rooks. Nor is there room for the story of the ugly goldfish, which I hope would deeply affect you. There is not even room to put in a few frosted spiders' webs, and no book, surely, can be regarded as complete unless at some point or other its pages are hung with frosted spiders' webs.

254

Worst of all, there is not even room to tell you about The Most Beautiful Flower in the World. It is not a rose; it is not an orchid, nor an iris, nor a wild flower, nor is it like any lily you have ever seen. It is my special secret.

But the bowl is full.

So there is nothing for it but to start another bowl, one of these days, and that, I am afraid, may mean writing yet another book.

Well . . . you have been warned.

BIBLIOGRAPHY OF WORKS BY BEVERLEY NICHOLS

This bibliography was prepared by Roy C. Dicks, retired reference librarian from the Wake County, North Carolina, Public Library System. Gratefully acknowledged are the earlier bibliographies prepared for the Nichols entry in *Contemporary Authors*, New Revision Series, Volume 17 (Gale Research 1986), and for the biography *Beverley Nichols: A Life* by Bryan Connon (Constable 1990).

Titles are arranged chronologically. UK publishers are listed first; US, if any, second. All entries refer to original editions; subsequent paper editions or reprints are not included.

NOVELS

Prelude (Chatto and Windus 1920)
Patchwork (Chatto and Windus 1921; Holt 1922)
Self (Chatto and Windus 1922)
Crazy Pavements (Jonathan Cape 1927; Doran 1927)
Evensong (Jonathan Cape 1932; Doubleday 1932)
Revue (Jonathan Cape 1939; Doubleday 1939)

MYSTERIES

No Man's Street (Hutchinson 1954; Dutton 1954)
The Moonflower (Hutchinson 1955; Dutton 1955 as
   The Moonflower Murder)
Death to Slow Music (Hutchinson 1956; Dutton 1956)
The Rich Die Hard (Hutchinson 1957; Dutton 1958)
Murder by Request (Hutchinson 1960; Dutton 1960)

SHORT STORIES

Women and Children Last (Jonathan Cape 1931; Doubleday 1931)
Men Do Not Weep (Jonathan Cape 1941; Harcourt 1942)

CHILDREN'S NOVELS

*The Tree That Sat Down (Jonathan Cape 1945)
*The Stream That Stood Still (Jonathan Cape 1948)
  These two titles were published in one volume by St. Martin's in 1966.
The Mountain of Magic (Jonathan Cape 1950)
The Wickedest Witch in the World (W. H. Allen 1971)

AUTOBIOGRAPHY

Twenty-Five (Jonathan Cape 1926; Doran 1926)
All I Could Never Be (Jonathan Cape 1949; Dutton 1952)
The Sweet and Twenties (Weidenfeld and Nicolson 1958)
A Case of Human Bondage (Secker and Warburg 1966; Award Books 1966)
Father Figure (Heinemann 1972; Simon and Schuster 1972)
Down the Kitchen Sink (W. H. Allen 1974)
The Unforgiving Minute (W. H. Allen 1978)

GARDENS AND HOMES

*Down the Garden Path (Jonathan Cape 1932; Doubleday 1932)
*A Thatched Roof (Jonathan Cape 1933; Doubleday 1933)
*A Village in a Valley (Jonathan Cape 1934; Doubleday 1934)
  These three titles form the Allways trilogy about Nichols' Tudor cottage in Glatton, Cambridgeshire. *The Gift of a Garden*, a condensation of the three, along with a new introduction by Nichols, was published by W. H. Allen in 1971 and Dodd in 1972.

How Does Your Garden Grow? (Allen and Unwin 1935; Doubleday 1935)
A collection of four radio essays by Nichols plus essays by Compton Mackenzie, Marion Cran and Vita Sackville-West.

Green Grows the City (Jonathan Cape 1939; Harcourt 1939)
About Nichols' city garden and contemporary home in Hampstead in greater London.

*Merry Hall (Jonathan Cape 1951; Dutton 1953)

*Laughter on the Stairs (Jonathan Cape 1953; Dutton 1954)

*Sunlight on the Lawn (Jonathan Cape 1956; Dutton 1956)
These three titles form the Merry Hall trilogy about Nichols' Georgian manor house in Ashtead, Surry. *The Gift of a Home*, a condensation of the three, along with a new introduction by Nichols, was published by W. H. Allen in 1972 and Dodd in 1973.

*Garden Open Today (Jonathan Cape 1963; Dutton 1963)

*Forty Favourite Flowers (Studio Vista 1964; St. Martin's 1965)

*Garden Open Tomorrow (Heinemann 1968; Dodd 1969)
These three titles form the Sudbrook trilogy about Nichols' late-eighteenth-century attached cottage in Richmond, Surrey.

The Art of Flower Arrangement (Collins 1967; Viking 1967)
Discusses the public use and social influence of flowers throughout history, covering a number of species.

POLITICS

Cry Havoc! (Jonathan Cape 1933; Doubleday 1933)

News of England; or a Country without a Hero (Jonathan Cape 1938; Doubleday 1938)

Verdict on India (Jonathan Cape 1944; Harcourt 1944)

Uncle Samson (Evans 1950)

RELIGION

The Fool Hath Said (Jonathan Cape 1936; Doubleday 1936)
A Pilgrim's Progress (Jonathan Cape 1952)

TRAVEL

No Place Like Home (Jonathan Cape 1936; Doubleday 1936)
The Sun in My Eyes (Heinemann 1969)

DRAMA

Failures (Jonathan Cape 1933)
    A collection of three plays: *The Stag, Avalanche,* and *When the Crash Comes.*
Evensong (Samuel French 1933)
    Written with Edward Knoblock.
Mesmer (Jonathan Cape 1937)
Shadow of the Vine (Jonathan Cape 1949)

MISCELLANEOUS

Memories and Melodies (Thornton Butterworth 1925; G. H. Doran 1926)
    Nichols "ghost-wrote" this "autobiography" of Dame Nellie Melba. The 1980 reissue of this title in Australia (Thomas Nelson) and in London (HamishHamilton) acknowledged Nichols' authorship.
*Are They the Same at Home? (Jonathan Cape 1927; Doran 1927)
*The Star-Spangled Manner (Jonathan Cape 1928; Doubleday 1928)
    These two books of celebrity sketches were published, together with *Twenty-Five,* as *Oxford—London—New York* by Jonathan Cape in 1931, with a new introduction by Nichols.

For Adults Only (Jonathan Cape 1932; Doubleday 1933)
 A satire on parental advice manuals.

Puck at Brighton: The Official Handbook of the County Borough of Brighton (Brighton Corporation Publicity Committee 1933)
 Annual tourist guide to which Nichols heavily contributed.

A Book of Old Ballads (Hutchinson 1934)
 Compiled and annotated by Nichols.

Yours Sincerely (George Newnes 1949)
 A collection of Nichols' columns from the popular weekly *Woman's Own*, including those by fellow columnist Monica Dickens.

The Queen's Coronation Day: The Pictorial Record of the Historic Occasion, with the Eyewitness Account of Her Majesty's Crowning (Pitkin Pictorials 1953)

Beverley Nichols' Cat Book (Thomas Nelson 1955)

*Beverely Nichols' Cats' A. B. C. (Jonathan Cape 1960; Dutton 1960)

*Beverley Nichols' Cats' X. Y. Z. (Jonathan Cape 1961; Dutton 1961)
 These two titles were published together as *Beverley Nichols' Cats' A to Z* in 1977 by W. H. Allen.

Powers That Be (Jonathan Cape 1966; St. Martin's 1966)
 An overview of paranormal phenomenon.

Twilight: First and Probably Last Poems (Bachman and Turner 1982)

BOOKS INTRODUCED OR PREFACED BY NICHOLS

The Faro Table, or The Gambling Mothers by Charles Sedley (Nash and Grayson 1931)

The Making of a Man: Letters from an Old Parson to His Sons by Albert Victor Baillie (Nicholson and Watson 1934)

BIBLIOGRAPHY OF WORKS

Cats in Camera by Jan Styczynski (Deutsch 1962)

In an Eighteenth Century Kitchen: A Receipt Book of Cookery, 1698 (Woolf 1968)
  A reprint of the original that Nichols found boarded up in his Glatton cottage and described in *A Thatched Roof*.

So Brief a Dream by Rafaelle, Duchess of Leinster (W. H. Allen 1973; John Day 1973 as *The Dutchess from Brooklyn*)

All About Cats (Orbis 1975)

Jam Tomorrow: Some Early Reminiscences by Basil Bartlett (Elek 1978)

INDEX

The index of plant names was prepared by Roy C. Dicks. Plants are indexed by currently accepted botanical name. A cross-reference has been provided wherever the author used a common name or outdated Latin name.

.

William McLaren
MCMLVI